PRAISE FOR

# LEADERSHIP REVOLUTION

The impact of John Perkins and Wayne Gordon on low-income urban communities has been profound. We in the business community can learn a lot from the leadership example and practices of these two servant leaders. Read this book and be inspired to make a difference.

**DAVID BERÉ**
CEO of Nonni's Food Group
Chairman of the Fuller Seminary Board of Trustees

When I think about John and Wayne, two important qualities of leadership stand above the rest: they listen and they take risks. These qualities have enabled them to become great friends and partners and to make a difference for thousands—if not millions—of people. These guys know leadership, and I know that reading this book will make a difference in your life.

**CAREY CASEY**
CEO of the National Center for Fathering

While most of Christian leadership material originates in the context of suburban, middle-class realities, these two ministry pioneers share hard-earned leadership lessons from the context of under-resourced communities that will equip thousands of Christian Community Development practitioners and leaders throughout the nation.

**NOEL CASTELLANOS**
CEO of Christian Community Development Association

John Perkins and Wayne Gordon are two of the wisest and greatest leaders I know. For nearly 20 years, I have been learning everything I can from them. This book is the newest, freshest fruit of the lifelong friendship of this dynamic duo of urban ministry.

**SHANE CLAIBORNE**
Author, Activist and Founding Partner of The Simple Way, Philadelphia, Pennsylvania

John Perkins and Wayne Gordon are unique visionary leaders who always write out of the heart of their firsthand and risk-taking leadership experiences. It is for that reason that the timely lessons they provide in *Leadership Revolution* can be trusted and adopted by those seeking to use their leadership gifts to create transformational and revolutionary change.

**LEAH GASKIN FITCHUE**
President of the Payne Theological Seminary, Wilberforce, Ohio

This inspiring and instructive book on leadership will be a lasting legacy from these two pioneers of faith-based community development. *Leadership Revolution* serves as a clarion call for a new generation of courageous Christians to embrace the cross, follow Christ, and take risks for God's kingdom.

**MARSHALL E. HATCH, SR.**
Senior Pastor of New Mount Pilgrim Missionary Baptist Church, Chicago, Illinois

I have known John and Wayne for more than three decades. They take servant leadership to a level I have rarely seen demonstrated. Their book is packed full of practical counsel for leaders. I loved it!

**BILL HYBELS**
Senior Pastor of Willow Creek Community Church, South Barrington, Illinios

John Perkins teaches us about Moses. Wayne Gordon teaches us about Nehemiah. Both of them teach us about Jesus. The principle of servant leadership is universal. *Leadership Revolution* is an excellent book that will be very helpful to me in my ministry.

**PATRICK MCCASKEY**
Senior Director of Special Projects for the Chicago Bears Football Club, Chicago, Illinois

John Perkins and Wayne Gordon have penned a book on leadership that is theologically sound, biblically consistent, and practically useful. This is an absolute must-read for the committed practitioner as well as the serious student of leadership.

**DAVID SVEEN**
President of Cedarstone Partners
Adjunct Assistant Professor at Wheaton College, Wheaton, Illinois

# LEADERSHIP REVOLUTION

## DEVELOPING THE VISION & PRACTICE OF FREEDOM & JUSTICE

JOHN M. PERKINS
& Wayne Gordon
WITH RANDALL FRAME

Regal

Published by Regal
From Gospel Light
Ventura, California, U.S.A.
www.regalbooks.com
Printed in the U.S.A.



Library of Congress Cataloging-in-Publication Data
Gordon, Wayne.
Leadership revolution : developing the vision and practice of freedom and justice / Wayne Gordon, John Perkins.
p. cm.
Includes bibliographical references and index.
ISBN 978-0-8307-6400-6 (trade paper : alk. paper)
1. Christian leadership. 2. Leadership—Religious aspects—Christianity.
I. Perkins, John, 1930- . II. Title.
BV652.1.G67 2012
253—dc23
2012025237

# APPRECIATION

*To the people of Lawndale and Mississippi, who have taught us far more than we have taught them.*

---

*We want to thank our wives for partnering with us: Vera Mae, 61 years; and Anne, 35 years; who have stood with us in all of life's endeavors.*

*Thanks to our children for teaching us so much through their living of life with us. The Perkins children: Spencer (deceased) and Nancy; Joanie and husband, Ron; Phillip and wife, Eva; Derek and wife, Karyn; Deborah, Wayne, Pricilla and Elizabeth. The Gordon children: Angela; Andrew and wife, Stacy; and Austin.*

*Special thanks to the fabulous people and staff of Lawndale Christian Community Church and ministries. Particular gratitude for all the staff and volunteers of the Spencer Perkins Center.*

*Thanks to the CCDA board and members for living out Christian Community Development with us.*

*We are thankful to Regal Books and Gospel Light's marvelous and supportive people: Bill Greig, Steve Lawson, Mark Weising and Alexis Spencer-Byers for making this book project a priority and helping it come to fruition.*

*We are indebted to Randy Frame for helping organize our thoughts and put words to our heartfelt beliefs. He had an amazing ability to craft our life's work of leadership into a manuscript.*

*We are also so thankful for our friendship for the last 30 years. It has enriched us both immensely, and we are eternally blessed to be deep personal friends.*

*John Perkins and Wayne Gordon*

# CONTENTS

# PREFACE

Several years ago, a wealthy older couple, pleased with something I had written, wanted to reward me by taking me out to a nice restaurant. As it turned out, this place was a little too nice for the likes of me. I showed up wearing a new pair of slacks and a button-down shirt. But this was a "jackets-only" establishment, and I hadn't brought one.

Fortunately, the restaurant kept a few extra suit coats in stock for the uninitiated. So I got in. But the evening had pretty much been ruined. I felt completely out of my element. No matter how often I checked, I was sure there was spinach lodged in my teeth or gravy dripping down my chin. I didn't know which fork to use when. (I still don't.) And I felt that every word I said was being analyzed for appropriateness.

I suspect that most people can relate to this feeling of complete discomfort when in certain situations or in the company of certain individuals (some of whom might be related to you through marriage). I'm happy to say that I feel completely the opposite when I'm with Wayne Gordon and John Perkins. Each of these guys is the kind of person who makes everyone around him feel not just welcome, but relevant and important. They're also the kind of people who, no matter how great the challenge, will not run from it. Instead, they move forward with the conviction that everything is going to be okay.

This attitude and this approach, I believe, lie at the core of successful leadership. For ultimately it doesn't matter how many leadership principles a person knows, or how many seminars he or she has attended, if that person is not someone whom others want to follow wholeheartedly.

The story of the friendship between John and Wayne, who is better known as "Coach" to most of those closest to him, is a remarkable one. Back in the mid-1970s, John became Coach's hero and mentor, as something in what the civil rights veteran was teaching and envisioning about Christian community development struck a chord with the young college graduate who felt God's call to minister in the tough neighborhood of North Lawndale in Chicago. It didn't take long for John to go from hero and mentor to colleague and friend. Decades later, each man—one an African American in his early eighties and the

other a white guy in his late fifties—considers the other his best friend. They talk by phone practically every other day, and, though they live hundreds of miles apart, they see each other several times a year. Demographically speaking, such a "best friendship" is at least very rare, if not one of a kind.

Combined, John and Wayne have 80 years of experience ministering in low-income urban and rural communities. More to the point, they have 80 years of experience training men and women from those communities to become effective leaders—of churches, ministries, businesses and other types of organizations. Their biblically based approach to leadership and leadership development is something that Christian leaders (and according to both Coach and John, everyone is a leader of someone) need not just to hear, but also to embrace and practice.

Some perceive that John is the theoretician, while Wayne is the practitioner. This perception, while not entirely inaccurate, is misleading. It's true that it was John who developed the philosophy of Christian community development—a philosophy built on the "3 Rs" (relocation, reconciliation and redistribution) and rooted in the concept that the people who have the problems are in the best position to solve them. It's also true that it was Coach who, in John's words, "helped live out my dream." Indeed, today Lawndale Community Church (where Wayne serves as Lead Pastor) oversees a multimillion-dollar budget. The church's ministries include a health center, a development corporation and a legal center. All this began in 1978 with 15 young people and a guy whose only aspiration was to teach high school, coach sports, and make disciples for Christ among young men in a rugged urban neighborhood.

What many don't appreciate is that John is not just a theoretician, and Wayne is not just a practitioner. For John and his wife, Vera Mae, the practice of Christian community development preceded the philosophy, as they relocated in 1960 from California to their Mississippi homeland to help alleviate poverty and oppression. Meanwhile, Wayne and his wife, Anne, have developed a very detailed theology of wholistic ministry—a theology he's shared with thousands of like-minded ministry leaders over the years, mostly under the auspices of the Christian Community Development Association (a network of individual and organizational Christian community development practitioners that was founded by John, Wayne and a few others in 1989).

Wayne considers the story of Lawndale Community Church to be as much John's story as his own. When the church formed an advisory board in 1984, John was the first person on it. And no major decision has ever been made by the church without first consulting John Perkins.

In sum, Coach and John have long spoken with one voice, and that is what they do in these pages. It's been my honor to assist them. The Church desperately needs leaders who practice what they preach. It also needs leaders—such as John Perkins and Wayne Gordon—who preach what they practice.

Randall L. Frame

CHAPTER ONE

# A CALL TO REVOLUTION

In the spring of 2012, we (John and Wayne) took a tour of Lawndale Community Church's newest building, the Lawndale Christian Health and Fitness Center—a gleaming facility housing 40 treadmills, 30 elliptical machines, an aerobics room spacious enough for a class of 100, a weight room, a running track, and a basketball court. One of the building's four floors is home to a pediatric health center featuring 15 dentist chairs and 15 examination rooms—a facility that will provide dental, vision and medical care for thousands of children in the years to come. There's also a café, featuring healthy foods. Still another floor, in addition to space appropriate for meetings and conference events, houses a women's health center.

As impressive as it is, the building itself pales in comparison to the view from its fourth-floor Skyline Room. This vantage point, as the name implies, features an unobstructed view of the Chicago skyline. But more importantly, from this window we can see buildings occupying four full blocks of Chicago's Ogden Avenue—buildings that represent what the people of Lawndale Community Church (LCC) have accomplished over the last 30-plus years.

On that beautiful spring day in 2012, we could see Hope House, which since 1995 has served as a temporary home to more than 3,000 men striving to overcome addiction to drugs or alcohol. We also saw our health center, which has provided affordable medical care for more than 140,000 patients. We saw our development corporation, which has provided some $50 million worth of affordable housing for people who desperately needed it. Over the years, we have helped more than 400 families purchase homes, and we operate more than 400 rental units, including the Dr. King Legacy Apartments, constructed on the very site where Dr. Martin Luther King Jr. lived when he operated out of Chicago in 1966.

We looked out at our gym building, whose facilities are used by more than 1,000 people each week. Nearby is Lou Malnati's Pizzeria, which not only provides community residents with an option for a delicious meal, but has also been a place where people who are trying to change directions in life can gain valuable job experience. We could see our Learning Center, which has provided supplemental educational opportunities (such as tutoring services) for countless people, mostly children and youth, over the years. We caught a glimpse of our legal

center, which offers affordable services for those who would otherwise have to face their trials alone (sometimes literally). We looked down on the fruit stand operated by Hope Fruit, one of a handful of new businesses established by the people of the church. Hope Fruit's roster of employees is at three and counting. And we could see the John and Vera Mae Perkins Center, where we meet each week for Sunday School, and where seminarians gather for classes in community development in partnership with Northern Seminary.

DESPITE THE ABSENCE OF BUILDINGS, ORGANIZED MINISTRIES, AND A DETAILED STRATEGIC PLAN, THERE WAS AN ABUNDANCE OF VISION AND ENERGY AND HOPE.

As we surveyed all of these buildings, each representing one or more ministries of the church, I (John) reflected back on one of my first visits to Lawndale some 30 years ago. At that time, I couldn't help laughing at how little there was to see—a weight machine, a couple of storefronts, a few dilapidated buildings, a handful of teenage kids just hangin' out, wondering what was going on, and this crazy young white guy with his wife, who said he was responding to a call from God.

I (Wayne) remember how John laughed at me back then, but I wasn't offended by it. I knew that his was a positive kind of laughter, not the sarcastic kind. For even in that early visit, he could see what most others could not. Despite the absence of buildings, organized ministries, and a detailed strategic plan, he sensed an abundance of vision and energy and hope. He had a strong sense that the Lord was going to do a great work not just *for* North Lawndale, but, more significantly, *through the people* of North Lawndale.

To say that Lawndale Community Church has experienced a transformation over the past three decades is a monumental understatement. At the core of this transformation is a philosophy of leadership that we consider to be revolutionary. It's a philosophy that John has passed on to me (Wayne), and that we both have passed on (and continue to pass on) to many others. We believe that the successful

transformation of those communities that are regarded as part of America's "underclass" (as well as the spiritual health and wellbeing of more affluent communities) requires an approach to leadership that is both solidly biblical and completely revolutionary. The goal of this book is to share and promote this approach to leadership in the hope of sparking and feeding a leadership revolution.

## Elements of the Revolution

We unapologetically advocate the approach commonly known as "servant leadership." As we will see, servant leadership differs starkly from a "top down" approach according to which the boss—he (or she) who must be obeyed—simply tells everyone else what to do. We believe not only that servant leadership is the most solidly rooted biblical model of leadership, but also that it constitutes a core component of the leadership revolution we seek. We are not talking here about doing things for others all the time. When we speak of servant leadership, we have in mind a commitment to sharing authority—to developing the people around us and empowering them to lead.

SERVANT LEADERSHIP CONSTITUTES A CORE COMPONENT OF THE LEADERSHIP REVOLUTION WE SEEK.

This book's emphasis not only on leadership but also on developing leaders sets it apart from much of the teaching on leadership that is currently available. The influence of too many effective leaders—however positive or profound their leadership might be—disappears almost instantly when the leader either moves on to some other challenge or dies, making it difficult to sustain a particular direction or endeavor.

We will make the case that if the Church of Jesus Christ is to experience a much-needed leadership revolution, the centerpiece of that

revolution must be a strong commitment to developing leaders from among those who surround us and with whom we interact on a regular basis. Leadership development is particularly crucial to the growth and healing of communities—both urban and rural—that have been ravaged by the related pathologies of homelessness, joblessness, crime, and drug and alcohol addiction. In fact, we will argue that a commitment to leadership development as a top priority ought to be considered an essential component of leadership.

Most of the examples and illustrations we use will come from a context with which both of us are intimately familiar: Lawndale Community Church and the North Lawndale neighborhood that the church is seeking to transform. However, we firmly believe that the attitudes, principles and policies we recommend are applicable to all who seek to become more effective as leaders and as developers of leaders, regardless of ministry setting or specific ministry goals. Our approach is grounded in Scripture, with a particular focus on Jesus Christ as the quintessential model of a developer of leaders.

## Defining the Barriers

Numerous factors conspire to prevent young men and women in neighborhoods such as North Lawndale from becoming the kinds of leaders they could be—the kinds of leaders their communities desperately need. Among the most significant factors is the breakdown of the family.

The late Millard Fuller, who founded Habitat for Humanity, used to tell the story of a house-building project in Atlanta. Habitat for Humanity had spent a couple of weeks building new homes on an entire block. As is still the case today, the organization's philosophy called for those who would be living in the homes to work, if able, alongside the Habitat volunteers. For this particular project, former president Jimmy Carter was among the volunteers.

Several weeks after the work was completed, Millard found himself in the neighborhood and decided to drive through to see how the houses looked and how things were going. A young boy about seven years of age was outside playing in the yard of the house that Jimmy

Carter had helped build. Millard rolled down his window, called the boy over, and asked him how he liked his new house.

"I love it," the boy responded.

Millard followed up with the question: "You know who helped build your house, don't you?"

Beaming from ear to ear, the boy responded, "Yes. My dad!"

Millard was slightly humbled, but mostly he was inspired by the realization that the man who had once led the free world meant very little to this young boy in comparison to his own father.

Unfortunately, not all young boys and girls have a dad like the father of the boy in this anecdote. It is far more common for children in inner cities across America not to know who their fathers are. Or perhaps the only time they see their dads is when they visit them in prison. Nearly 90 percent of all babies born in Lawndale are born to single mothers. Single parents head 75 percent of the families in our neighborhood. According to one study, children born to unwed teen high school dropouts are 10 times more likely than other children to be living in poverty by the time they finish grade school.

Many of the qualities associated with good leaders have their roots in stable families where children find love, security and affirmation. Those for whom the proper emotional and spiritual groundwork has not been laid are up against tremendous odds. That is to say, young people who come from unstable families will find it very difficult to develop into strong, godly leaders. Among other challenges, many of these children will grow up without access to people who can model the attitudes and skills required for effective leadership at virtually any level. Absent intervention of some sort, these children are more likely to end up in prison than they are to become leaders. Beyond all this, we are up against cultural values according to which marriage is not the sacred institution it once was. In fact, today in the United States, there are more unmarried than married adults.

The problems that plague what sociologist William Julius Wilson has labeled the "underclass" are so numerous and interrelated that it's difficult to pinpoint any one of them as being more significant or fundamental than the others in terms of inhibiting the development of leaders. Some have pointed to substandard educational systems. It certainly is difficult for people to become leaders when they can't read

above a fifth or sixth grade level. The systems in most cities are in such poor shape that children typically "check out" by grade 5 even if they don't officially drop out until grade 10 or 11.

The challenges facing inner-city schools have been reasonably well documented. Academic achievement is often low, disruptive behavior is common, and teacher morale is so low that it's not unusual for teachers to simply not show up. On an average morning in Chicago, more than 5,000 children come to school only to find that they have no teacher that day. Much of what urban children and youth learn, they learn in the street. In school, they are not learning even basic life skills, let alone what they need to become leaders in their homes and communities. Instead of developing what sociologists call "prosocial" (as opposed to "antisocial") behavior, these children are, by default, majoring in survival skills. All too often, these survival skills include a propensity to violence.

ON AN AVERAGE MORNING IN CHICAGO, MORE THAN 5,000 CHILDREN COME TO SCHOOL ONLY TO FIND THAT THEY HAVE NO TEACHER THAT DAY.

Some have cited a lack of meaning in life as the primary root of the problem. Cornel West addresses this issue in his classic work, *Race Matters*:

> We have created rootless, dangling people with little link to the supportive networks family, friends, school that sustain some sense of purpose in life. We have witnessed the collapse of the spiritual communities that in the past helped Americans face despair, disease, and death and that transmit through the generations dignity and decency, excellence and elegance.[1]

The inability to find meaning in life causes people to lose hope. Without hope, many turn to drugs, which in turn contributes to an

epidemic of crime, including violent crime. Drug abuse accounts for an overwhelming percentage of the violent crime in North Lawndale.

Racism, both historical and current, is a major contributing factor to urban decay. Minorities have faced discrimination on many fronts, including in the areas of hiring and housing laws and policies. In addition, persons of color have often had limited access to the leadership advice, wisdom, and "nuts and bolts" knowledge that is readily accessible to members of the majority culture.

Poor economic conditions have also contributed to the problem, as young people who find their employment options limited are lured into the seemingly lucrative drug-dealing culture. At the same time, many of those who make up the underclass have come to be overly dependent on government programs that have produced unintended consequences, including the gradual decline of the work ethic that characterized previous generations of urban poor.

## Flight from Blight

In a tragic twist, the migration of black professionals away from poorer neighborhoods—a phenomenon made possible by the desegregation efforts of the civil rights movement—has contributed to the dearth of leadership in blighted urban communities. There was a time when black people—regardless of their accomplishments, abilities and educational levels—because of discriminatory housing laws and policies had no choice but to remain in the ghetto. The upside to this unjust reality was that many positive role models—doctors, lawyers, schoolteachers, pastors, bus drivers, carpenters, electricians, and others—lived together in the same neighborhoods. But in recent decades, a high percentage of these potential role models have pursued their own personal and familial dreams and goals, leaving behind many of their former neighbors.

In the wake of this flight, young people have had few indigenous leaders after whom to model their lives. They have limited access to the simple, day-to-day lessons that most communities take for granted—things as basic as watching men and women go off to work each morning and coach young people's sports teams in the afternoon or evening.

In the preface to his book *The American Millstone*, James Squires introduced a new dynamic to the problem, as he wrote that those who are "hopelessly trapped in the urban centers of Chicago and other large cities" appear to have gained "political and social acceptance as a permanent fixture of the world's most advanced society without much understanding of, or concern about, the consequences."[2] Hence the term "permanent underclass."

Witnessing what has transpired in hundreds if not thousands of communities across the United States is a discouraging exercise, particularly to people—including me (John)—who decades ago marched, demonstrated, and on many occasions risked our lives so that African Americans and other ethnic minorities would no longer have to live as "second class" citizens—so that they, like all Americans, would have an uncluttered path to life, liberty, and the pursuit of happiness.

ALL THE NEGATIVE CONTRIBUTING FACTORS INTERACT WITH THE OTHERS—RESULTING IN AN ENVIRONMENT LESS THAN CONDUCIVE TO THE DEVELOPMENT OF LEADERS.

While it's important to recognize and understand the challenges facing many of our young people today, ultimately, determining which factors are most responsible for the creation and maintenance of a permanent underclass is not the issue. The truth is that all the negative contributing factors interact with the others—and among the results is an environment that is less than conducive to the development of leaders.

Ironically, the very thing these communities need if they are to find healing is effective leadership—men and women who will use their God-given talents, work to develop their leadership skills, and make a long-term commitment to loving and serving with pride whatever community each calls "home." For this to happen will require a leadership revolution. The success of this revolution will depend largely on the commitment current leaders make to developing other leaders around them.

Unfortunately, some youth with natural leadership ability and a willingness to lead have emerged as leaders of local street gangs, which typically end up being landing places for urban youth who crave a place to belong and who are looking for someone—anyone—to follow.

On the positive side, the Church—and the African-American Church in particular—presents an alternative opportunity for people to lead. North Lawndale is home to some 180 churches, though most of their pastors do not live in the areas where their churches are located. Historically the Black Church has functioned as a great nurturer of leaders—a venue wherein leaders and aspiring leaders have found a place to exercise their gifts and skills. It is no wonder that so many of those who went on to become great leaders of American society—people such as Reverend Adam Clayton Powell Jr., Reverend Dr. Martin Luther King Jr., and Reverend Jesse Jackson—were nurtured in the crucible of the Church. Though the prestige of the Black Church (and the American Church at large) has to some extent waned over time, black pastors by and large are still highly respected leaders in the African-American community.

THE BLACK CHURCH HAS FUNCTIONED AS A NURTURER OF LEADERS—A VENUE WHEREIN LEADERS HAVE FOUND A PLACE TO EXERCISE THEIR GIFTS AND SKILLS.

## Proclaiming Hope

As followers of Jesus Christ, we believe that the hope for the renewal of our neighborhoods and our communities—and ultimately of our nation and our world—lies with the Body of Christ—the Church. Even in the midst of despair, the Church must continue to proclaim life and hope.

Today, the Church hungers for leaders committed to carrying the light of Christ to the lives of individuals and to bringing biblical values to the structures of our society. Those of us who already are leaders must not be content merely to lead. It's time for us to make a firm

commitment to leadership development—the linchpin strategy of the revolution.

To this end, we hope that this book will serve not only to proclaim a prophetic word but also as a source of both Scripture-based wisdom and practical advice. Let the leadership revolution begin!

**Notes**

1. Cornel West, *Race Matters* (Boston, MA: Beacon Press, 2001), p. 5.
2. James D. Squires, ed., *The American Millstone* (Chicago, IL: Contemporary Books, 1986).

CHAPTER TWO

# ROOTS OF THE REVOLUTION

For more than 30 years now, John has poured his life into my (Wayne's) life and into the life of Lawndale Community Church. He travels to Lawndale at least five or six times a year. He's been present at many of Lawndale's major events and has cut the ribbon at quite a few dedication ceremonies.

Besides being a fixture in the community, John has also become a cherished member of my family—my three children refer to him as "Grandpa Perkins." Indeed, John's mark on their lives is unmistakable. "Granddaughter" Angela now teaches in the same Chicago public school she once attended and is the co-director of Lawndale's summer education program. While in college, "Grandson" Andrew started Hope Fencing, which several years later is still a thriving business in Lawndale. Now a Chicago business professional, he continues to care deeply about people and justice issues. "Grandson" Austin, the entrepreneur behind Hope Fruit, has every intention of participating in Lawndale's continuing transformation and developing as a leader. (As we will see, commitments to remain in the community and to accept the responsibility to lead are essential roots of the revolution.)

In short, John lives out Paul's instructions to his protégé in 2 Timothy 2:2: "And the things you have heard me say in the presence of many witnesses entrust to reliable men [and women] who will also be qualified to teach others." This verse lies at the core of the leadership revolution. Clearly, it speaks to the transmission of knowledge, experience and wisdom from those who have learned to those who are learning. It also calls for selfless sharing for the sake of others' growth and, ultimately, for the benefit of the kingdom of God.

We will speak frequently in this book of the importance of leaders "pouring their lives" into others. When we use this phrase, we have in mind both 2 Timothy 2:2 and our own experience of friendship, mentoring and shared ministry. The leadership revolution's success will depend on current leaders first identifying future leaders and then molding them by pouring their lives into them.

Before we delve into the specifics of the leadership revolution, it may be helpful to briefly review some of the commonly held wisdom on what constitutes effective leadership. In other words, what does a good leader look like?

## Leadership Defined

John Maxwell, one of the most widely read and highly regarded authorities on the topic, defines "leadership" with a single word: "influence." We agree, though we'd like to modify this definition somewhat. Consider a ruthless dictator who has the backing of a well-armed military regime with the authority to use whatever force is required to squelch dissent. This dictator wields great influence. But is he a leader in the purest sense of the word?

GENUINE LEADERSHIP IS DEFINED
IN TERMS OF INFLUENCE THAT
IS WELCOMED AND DESIRED.

We suggest that genuine leadership is defined in terms of influence that is welcomed and desired, as opposed to influence achieved by brute force, psychological intimidation, or emotional manipulation. With this qualification in place, permission to lead is gained not through immoral or unethical means, but by such positive qualities as intelligence, charisma, hard work, concern for others, and moral vision. Remember that Jesus changed the course of history without any swords, guns, armies, or high-powered politicians behind Him.

Those who are striving to become better leaders would do well to recognize that leaders are not managers. In fact, many leaders, including yours truly (both of us), are very poor managers. In his book, *The Dynamics of Leadership*, Harold W. Reed notes that leadership is "asking the fundamental questions, while management is implementing the answers."[1] Some might find helpful Olan Hendrix's elaboration on the differences between leadership and management:

1. Leadership is a quality; management is a science and an art.
2. Leadership provides vision; management supplies realistic perspectives.
3. Leadership deals with concepts; management relates to functions.

4. Leadership exercises faith; management has to do with fact.
5. Leadership seeks for effectiveness; management strives for efficiency.
6. Leadership is an influence for good among potential resources; management is the coordination of available resources organized for maximum accomplishments.
7. Leadership provides direction; management is concerned about control.
8. Leadership thrives on finding opportunity; management succeeds on accomplishment.[2]

Another way of looking at these differences is to distinguish between things that are urgent and things that are important. Henri Nouwen counsels that if we allow our lives to be consumed by the urgent, we "will never do what is truly important and will always feel dissatisfied."[3]

Leaders know how to delegate "urgent" matters to those who are better equipped to handle them and to focus their efforts on what is truly important.

## Leadership Qualities

In order to gain new perspectives and to sharpen their skills, we strongly recommend that those who want to grow in their leadership abilities read as many books on leadership as they can, including those from authors such as Maxwell, Andy Stanley, Martin Luther King Jr., Madeleine Albright, Stephen Covey, Colin Powell, Jim Collins, Laurie Beth Jones, and others. Our purpose in this section is not to provide an exhaustive assessment, but rather an overview of the qualities generally associated with successful leadership.

First and, arguably, foremost, leaders are motivators; they are capable of getting others to follow. Effective leaders succeed at motivating for a variety of reasons. Some have engaging, charismatic personalities. Others motivate by identifying an important problem that needs to be solved and making an argument that's strong enough to get others to join in the effort to solve it.

In motivating others, good leaders recognize the wisdom in German writer Johann Wolfgang von Goethe's admonition: "Correction does

much, but encouragement does more." As a result, they make a conscious effort to identify both the strengths and the weaknesses of those who are following, including those being developed as leaders. Leaders help people find ways to build on their strengths and to work around or compensate for their weaknesses. Better yet, they help people turn their weaknesses into strengths. In short, leaders strive to bring out the best in others.

The best leaders are people of high moral and ethical character—people of integrity. They don't say one thing and do another. Those who cheat or deceive (especially if they do so for selfish purposes) might be able to con some folks into following them for a while, but not for the long haul. People follow those whom they trust. Those who demonstrate that they can't be trusted or who are guilty of significant moral failures compromise their ability to lead.

LEADERS HELP PEOPLE FIND WAYS TO BUILD ON THEIR STRENGTHS AND TO WORK AROUND OR COMPENSATE FOR THEIR WEAKNESSES.

On a related note, leaders are dependable. They say what they're going to do, and then they do it. They set reasonable goals, and they accomplish them. Leaders specialize in transformation—change for the better. They are problem solvers who are not afraid to ask for help if they need it, because accomplishing the goal trumps personal pride every time.

Leaders are tireless workers. In fact, they are willing to work at least as hard as they expect those following them to work. Their commitment to the cause is second to none.

Leaders are constantly growing—constantly seeking to improve their skills and increase their knowledge. They are good listeners, because they realize that we learn more when we listen than we do when we talk. They also understand that listening communicates to others that they are cared for and that their opinions and perspectives are being heard.

Leaders are people of vision. They believe that great things are possible, even when many or most others think they are not. With confidence and hope, they counteract the skepticism and cynicism of those who say it can't be done.

The best leaders are collaborators, not Lone Rangers. They bring people together around a common mission. They are readily open to the possibility that other people's ideas are better than theirs. The visions they pursue and the goals they seek to accomplish need not always be their own, but can belong to someone else or result from a team effort.

Leaders are effective communicators. If they have to, they "overcommunicate" in order to make sure there are as few surprises as possible, and that all who are part of the mission know everything they need to know in order to make their best contribution.

Leaders do not shy away from crisis. When something goes wrong, good leaders do not run away from the problem. They run toward it. Oftentimes, leadership qualities emerge and shine most brightly amid the darkness of a crisis. Perhaps the best contemporary example of this is the evolution of Rudy Giuliani from a so-so New York City mayor to a veritable hero in the days and months following the horror of 9/11.

WHEN SOMETHING GOES WRONG, GOOD LEADERS DO NOT RUN AWAY FROM THE PROBLEM. THEY RUN TOWARD IT.

A crisis, while it certainly has the potential to bring out the worst in people, can also bring out the best in followers as well as leaders. Highly respected former football coach Lou Holtz faced something of a crisis in 1978, when his Arkansas Razorbacks were about to face a better Oklahoma team in the Orange Bowl. He lost his best lineman to injury a week or so before the big game. Then he suspended his top two running backs for disciplinary reasons. Against all odds, Arkansas won the game: 31-6. When asked afterwards how they did it, Holtz commented that his team recognized the crisis and came together to face it head-on.

Leaders feel the pain and fear that accompany a crisis. They don't create or hope for pain or sorrow—but when it comes, they treat it as an opportunity for growth.

Finally, leaders are not perfect. We make mistakes, plenty of them. You will learn about a few of ours in the pages to come.

## Born or Made?

There is a longstanding debate between those who subscribe to the so-called trait theory of leadership and those who advocate the "process" theory. In other words, some maintain that leaders are born (with just the right traits), while others hold that leaders are made (through the process of developing the skills and perspectives associated with leadership).

To a large extent, we consider this debate to be artificial—a sort of exercise in futility—for it makes sense to conclude that both positions are accurate to some degree. Think about musicians and athletes. They are born with a certain amount of natural talent, whether a musical ear or the ability to run fast. But to develop whatever natural-born talent they have, both the musician and the athlete must commit to learning and practicing.

The same is true of leaders. Ultimately, it doesn't matter how much inborn ability a person has. What *does* matter is that everyone can improve. All people can become better leaders. This is not to say that everyone is capable of becoming a U.S. senator or a professional football coach. But just because a person is not the head of a major corporation doesn't mean he or she is not a leader. Throughout this book, we will promote the concept that virtually all people are leaders at some level, based on our capacity to influence others. People can—and should—become better leaders in every venue where they have the opportunity, including in their churches, communities and families.

Unfortunately, the lack of opportunity to lead—or to develop a solid social and emotional foundation in preparation for leadership—is often perceived as a lack of ability or potential. By and large, as noted in the introduction, those who comprise what has been referred to as the permanent underclass have simply not had sufficient access to the tools they need to become all they could be as leaders.

But we have seen too many people who "had no chance" grow into very significant positions of leadership to believe the myth that leaders can't be made. You'll meet a few of these people in these pages.

We can't change the past, but we *can* shape the future. The time to begin doing so is now. Not only do we believe that the ability to lead at any and all levels *can* be taught and learned, but we also believe it *must* be taught and learned if the leadership revolution is to succeed.

**Notes**

1. Harold W. Reed, *The Dynamics of Leadership* (Danville, IL: Interstate Printers & Publishers, 1982), p. 19.
2. Olan Hendrix, *Three Dimensions of Leadership* (St. Charles, IL: Churchsmart Resources, 2000).
3. Henri J.M. Nouwen, *The Road to Daybreak* (New York: Doubleday, 1990), p. 81.

CHAPTER THREE

# JESUS AS SERVANT LEADER

In 1969, I (John) spent some time in a jail in Mendenhall, Mississippi. I'd gone there to protest the mistreatment of black youth who had been imprisoned and beaten for alleged inappropriate behavior around white people, and I ended up getting arrested myself. Risking their own wellbeing, several dozen people, including Vera Mae, came to the jail to show their support. I spoke to them through a jail window.

It didn't take the group long to decide to engage in a boycott of the town's businesses. Vera Mae organized the effort. Young people made signs urging people not to shop in downtown Mendenhall. They took their efforts to the streets. The community got behind them. Items customers had put on layaway stayed there. People chose not to buy things they wanted (or perhaps needed) until justice was done.

Although these people probably would not have labeled it as such, they were practicing servant leadership. At the core of servant leadership is a willingness to sacrifice. Sacrifice presumes an attitude of humility—an approach to life that puts others above ourselves.

AT THE CORE OF SERVANT LEADERSHIP IS A WILLINGNESS TO SACRIFICE. SACRIFICE PRESUMES AN ATTITUDE OF HUMILITY—AN APPROACH TO LIFE THAT PUTS OTHERS ABOVE OURSELVES.

Jesus consistently modeled this kind of humility—sometimes in shocking ways, such as when He wrapped a towel around His waist and began to wash His disciples' feet as they sat down to the Passover meal (see John 13:2-5). It must have been extraordinary for the disciples to witness their Teacher—the long-awaited Messiah—performing a menial task usually assigned to a servant.

But really, they shouldn't have been surprised at all. Scripture makes it abundantly clear that Jesus had always modeled and taught a style of leadership whose goal was not to dominate or boss others around, but rather to humbly serve them.

In humility, Jesus submitted Himself to the baptism of John the Baptist, despite John's efforts to deter Him (see Matt. 3:13-17). He later

said to His apostles, "Whoever wants to become great among you must be your servant, and whoever wants to be first must be slave of all. For even the Son of Man did not come to be served, but to serve" (Mark 10:43-45). He also told them that "whoever exalts himself will be humbled, and whoever humbles himself will be exalted" (Matt. 23:12).

Eric Metaxas, in his biography of Dietrich Bonhoeffer, describes a radio address that Bonhoeffer, then a young theologian, delivered on February 1, 1933. The address had been planned for some time, but as things turned out, it was broadcast two days after Hitler came to power. In the address, Bonhoeffer refuted the Führer Principle—the concept that the Führer is in essence above the law, and that his will represents the collective will of the people. (Those who subscribe to this principle in effect give free reign to a dictator.) Metaxas writes, "The difference between real leadership and the false leadership of the Leader was this: real leadership derived its authority from God, the source of all goodness. . . . But the authority of the Führer was submitted to nothing. It was self-derived and autocratic, and therefore had a messianic aspect."[1]

Metaxas quotes Bonhoeffer (in the radio address) as saying, "The true Leader must always be able to disillusion. It is just this that is his responsibility and his real object. He must lead his following away from the authority of his person. . . . He must radically refuse to become the appeal, the idol, i.e. the ultimate authority of those whom he leads."[2]

Servant leaders refuse to allow themselves to be viewed as demigods or saints in the eyes of their followers, some of whom may be very impressionable. Taking advantage of those who are easily impressed is for cult leaders, not servant leaders. Servant leaders make it clear that they are less important than the mission. Godly leadership is not about attaining recognition or glory; it's about serving others. It's about being humble, not being the boss.

It can be tempting for leaders to develop a false sense of their own importance. There is no place for this if we are trying to create a culture in which new leaders are developed and nurtured. The senior pastor's name does not have to be on every church sign, nor does he or she have to be front and center on the church's website. This sends the message that the ministry is "mine," not "ours."

## On Not Getting Our Own Way

Being a servant leader means that sometimes—maybe more than just sometimes—the leader doesn't get what he or she wants. I (Wayne) have experienced this type of disappointment many times. On one occasion, I was convinced that it was in the best interests of our ministry to purchase a 2,000-seat theater. My mind ran wild thinking about the many things we could do with such a facility. However, others in leadership positions at Lawndale felt that the money we would have to spend to purchase and renovate the theater could be better invested in other projects.

The question of whether or not to buy the theater came to a vote. Everyone knew where I stood. They knew that I favored purchasing the theater. But they also knew that I wanted them to vote based on what they thought, not what I thought. I asked people to pray about the matter and seek God's will for our church.

When the votes were tallied, I lost. Even my wife voted not to buy the theater. I confess it took me awhile to get over this defeat. It was a bit of a blow to my pride. My natural reaction was to question whether I should still be leading the church.

BEING A SERVANT LEADER MEANS THAT SOMETIMES, THE LEADER DOESN'T GET WHAT HE OR SHE WANTS.

After a few days, however, I started to see the whole thing differently. I felt a sense of pride and accomplishment that other leaders at Lawndale felt complete freedom to disagree with me. I found it freeing to be reminded that it's not all about me. It's about all of us. I'm not in charge of everything. Ultimately, I don't want to be. Each of Lawndale's ministries—the health center, the development corporation, our Hope House recovery home, and several others—has its own leader. Influence is spread around—as opposed to being concentrated in the hands of one person, or even a few people. This is one of the keys to Lawndale's growth. We have many stakeholders—and people

tend to make better decisions when they have a stake in the matter. Truth be told, as time went on and we learned more about the building I'd wanted to buy, my enthusiasm waned. I became more and more convinced that the decision that had been made was the right one after all.

## Eliminating the Distance

Many leadership models assume—or even prescribe—a certain distance and detachment between leaders and those they lead. The beauty and challenge of servant leadership is that it eliminates that distance, whether the separation is social or created by organizational charts. Henri Nouwen, in his book *In The Name of Jesus*, comments poignantly on this topic:

> Somehow we have come to believe that good leadership requires a good distance from those we are called to lead. Medicine, psychiatry, and social work all offer us models in which service takes place in a one way direction. Someone serves, someone else is being served, and be sure not to mix up the roles! But how can anyone lay down their life for those with whom he is not even allowed to enter into a deep personal relationship? Laying down your life means making your own faith and doubt, hope and despair, joy and sadness, courage and fear available to others as ways of getting in touch with the Lord of life. We are not the healers, we are not the reconcilers, and we are not the givers of life. We are sinful broken vulnerable people who need as much care as anyone we care for.[3]

According to Nouwen, a leader is a vulnerable servant who needs people as much as they need him. Christian leadership is modeled not on the power games of the world but on the servant-leader Jesus, who came to give His life for the salvation of humankind. As a result, Christian leadership involves a softness and vulnerability that are not often found in business and organizational leadership structures, including those designated as "Christian."

The key to the servant leader's influence is not power, but the powerlessness that Jesus modeled for us. As Nouwen suggests, the temptation of power is greatest when people struggle to find intimacy. Leaders—even Christian leaders—who do not know how to develop healthy, intimate relationships often opt for power and control. Sadly, many a Christian empire has been built by people who were unable to give and receive love that went beneath the surface.

There's another kind of distance that servant leaders also strive to eliminate: the gap between what the leaders do and what they tell others to do. Servant leaders lead collaboratively, not dictatorially. They are more interested in inviting other people to walk alongside them than they are in getting other people to do things for them.

Several years ago, an employee at a Christian ministry, after about a week on the job, expressed to another employee his disappointment that the top executives got special privileges. The veteran employee asked the newcomer to clarify his remark. The new employee explained that he thought it sent the wrong signal that the two best parking spots in the lot were reserved for the ministry's leaders. "Every day I've been here," he said, "the only cars I've seen in those two best spots are the cars of the president and the vice-president."

His colleague then explained what was really going on: "Those spots are not reserved. Anyone can have them. The reason you always see the president and vice-president parking there is that they are the first ones to arrive in the morning and the last ones to leave at night."

Servant leaders do not need to tell others what to do; others know what is expected by the example that has been set. Leaders who are in right relationship with those who are following (or walking alongside) do not have to "pull rank" by appealing to the power vested in them by the organizational chart. Anyone who has to say, "Because I'm the boss" in response to a different viewpoint or opinion has already lost. Servant leaders lead based on the integrity of their character, their moral vision, and their commitment to serving others.

In our time, Mother Teresa represents the quintessential example of a servant leader. Physically small and weak—even frail—she held no title and had no corporate organizational structure behind her. She earned her influence by devoting her life to serving the most vulnerable people she could find on the streets of Calcutta, India. In the 1990s,

speaking at a Washington, DC, prayer breakfast in front of the nation's most powerful political leaders (including then-President Clinton), she spoke on behalf of unborn children, inviting all those considering abortion to give their children to her. How does someone with no title, no money, and no political connections earn the right to deliver a prophetic message on Capitol Hill? By demonstrating servant leadership.

## Willingness to Sacrifice

Servant leaders commit to making sacrifices and to identifying with the pain and agony of those they are leading and attempting to serve. They are willing to sacrifice in a number of areas, including their own agendas, career advancement, financial gain, and even personal safety. Jesus, the ultimate servant leader, gave His own life and challenged His followers to commit to giving everything they had, including their lives.

SERVANT LEADERS ARE WILLING TO SACRIFICE IN A NUMBER OF AREAS, INCLUDING THEIR OWN AGENDAS, CAREER ADVANCEMENT, FINANCIAL GAIN, AND EVEN PERSONAL SAFETY.

During the Civil Rights era, leaders had to make numerous sacrifices and take great risks to do what we believed needed to be done. In our work in Mendenhall, Mississippi, during those years, my wife, Vera Mae, and I (John) were willing to make those sacrifices and take those risks so we could improve things, not just for our own family, but also for others, many of whom were less fortunate than we were. We weren't the only ones who chose to lead in that way. On one occasion, I attended a meeting called by a young man who was seeking support for a demonstration he was organizing for the cause of freedom. He appealed not only to adults, but also to the youth to participate. He made sure everyone knew that he could guarantee nothing and could not predict what might happen. Not just the adults, but the

young people, too, could be beaten and jailed, perhaps even killed. As he finished his speech, he announced that if not even one other person chose to participate, he would still go. His willingness as a servant leader to sacrifice was enough to inspire my own children to commit to the cause.

Today, it's less common to see leaders of Christian ministries who are willing to sacrifice or take risks that could lead to suffering. In fact, some ministries actually revolve around the pursuit of personal comfort and material prosperity. Money and success have taken the place of the kind of sacrificial service that is required to truly make a difference in the lives of others.

Servant leaders give themselves to a cause no matter the cost. They subscribe to the philosophy that if a person hasn't found something he or she is ready to die for, that person hasn't really found anything worth living for. Their willingness to risk everything in service to God and people enables them to experience the peace that passes all understanding and the joy that awaits on the other side of suffering. Two wonderful examples of servant leaders are our wives, Anne and Vera Mae, who have faithfully lived out this sacrificial principle over the years, abandoning many of their own goals and dreams so that our respective ministry visions could thrive.

## On Falling Short

As much as we (John and Wayne) have sought to exemplify the humility that characterizes servant leadership, we acknowledge for the record that we have made mistakes and fallen short on more than one occasion. For example, we regret having our pictures—as leaders of the Christian Community Development Association (CCDA)—appear on the inside cover of a special edition *CEV* Bible produced by the American Bible Society. The presence of these photos gave the impression that CCDA was our personal fiefdom and that we were the top bosses—a perception we did not and do not want to convey.

Leaders, like their followers, make mistakes. When we do, it's important that we acknowledge them, fix them to the extent possible, apologize when necessary, and then move on.

## The Priority of Love

Everything that servant leadership is about can be summarized by a single word: love. Genuine love has no room for paternalism, which unfortunately has often characterized the approach of white evangelicals active in underprivileged communities. In subtle (and sometimes not-so-subtle) ways, paternalism makes it clear who's still in charge. In contrast, the love that springs from servant leadership results in the empowerment, training and discipling of others. It offers full rights, responsibilities and opportunities.

Scripture could not be clearer about the fact that Jesus' life on earth was completely dominated by a limitless love for people. Matthew 9:36 reads: "When he saw the crowds, he had compassion on them, because they were harassed and helpless, like sheep without a shepherd." In Mark 1:41, we see Jesus "filled with compassion" and healing the hand of a leper.

On several occasions, the Gospel writers describe Jesus as being hungry, worn, weary or sad—but never to the point where He doesn't have time for those who need Him. Matthew 14:12 tells of John the Baptist's disciples bringing Jesus the news of John's violent death. Undoubtedly deeply grieved, Jesus "withdrew by boat privately to a solitary place" (v. 13). But the crowds discovered His whereabouts and followed Him on foot. They wouldn't leave Him alone. What did Jesus do? He "had compassion on them and healed their sick" (v. 14).

Servant leaders demonstrate their love of others by committing their lives to them. Because of love, when they witness a young boy selling dope on the street, they see a vision of hope to bring to his life. Because of love, they come to the aid of a teen faced with an unwanted pregnancy, or a breadwinner who has been laid off, or a family that has lost a child or faces foreclosure on their home. If we as servant leaders begin by loving—truly loving—other people, we'll be amazed at how many ministry strategies and initiatives will line up and fall neatly into place.

**Notes**

1. Eric Metaxas, *Bonhoeffer: Pastor, Martyr, Prophet, Spy* (Nashville, TN: Thomas Nelson, 2010), p. 141.
2. Ibid.
3. Henri J.M. Nouwen, *In the Name of Jesus* (London: Darton Longman and Todd, 1989), pp. 43-44.

CHAPTER FOUR

# LEADERSHIP LESSONS FROM JESUS (PART 1)

One day, shortly after beginning His preaching ministry, Jesus went for a walk by the Sea of Galilee and spotted two fishermen—brothers Simon (Peter) and Andrew. He called them to follow Him, and they left their nets to become the first of His disciples (see Matt. 4:18-20). Then He came upon another pair of fishermen brothers—James and John. Once again, He called, and they followed (see vv. 21-22). In similar fashion, He extended an invitation to the tax collector, Levi, who also immediately "got up and followed him" (Mark 2:14).

Easily history's most influential, and most revolutionary, leader and developer of leaders, Jesus Christ attracted hundreds, perhaps even thousands, of followers during His short earthly ministry. He also provided, by His example, a rich repository of leadership principles for those of us who desire to follow Him today. If you ever take the time to read through the Gospels with a focus on Jesus' role as a leader and developer of leaders, you will likely be amazed at the valuable lessons available to be mined.

In this chapter, we will examine Jesus' attitudes and attributes as they relate to leadership development, while the following chapter will focus more on His behavior or actions. We make this distinction fully aware that the line between what a leader is like (attitude) and what a leader does (behavior) is by no means a solid one. In fact, people's attitudes and perspectives—the things they believe—are revealed by their actions—the things they say and do. Still, it seemed good to organize the insights we have gleaned by studying Jesus' approach to leadership in this way.

## Proactive

There are many words that can and should be used to describe Jesus. "Shy," "reserved" and "passive" are not among them. Jesus was overwhelmingly proactive. He knew that He would need other people to help Him carry out His mission here on earth—and He didn't wait for those people to come to Him. He went out and got them, as we have already seen.

The Bible gives a lot of attention to the "Twelve"—or the apostles—those who were especially close to Jesus. But Scripture also speaks often of disciples—followers of Jesus—who were not among the Twelve.

Luke 10:1 makes reference to Jesus sending out 72 of His followers. It's likely that many of these followers, even those who were not among the Twelve, were extremely close to Jesus. In Luke 24:1-8, we see that the apostles were not the first people to learn that Jesus had been raised from the dead.

JESUS KNEW HE WOULD NEED OTHER PEOPLE TO HELP HIM CARRY OUT HIS MISSION HERE ON EARTH—AND HE DIDN'T WAIT FOR THOSE PEOPLE TO COME TO HIM.

One gets the impression that wherever He went, Jesus invited people to follow Him. Besides the apostles and other named disciples, we find Him inviting one unnamed man after another to follow Him (see, for example, Luke 9:57-62). Not everyone accepts, but the invitation is always extended.

It's important to recognize that Jesus did not find His followers at leadership conferences or in the halls of academia. He didn't check to see whether or not they had seminary degrees or how well they had done on their standardized tests. He didn't even ask for references. He didn't put out the word far and wide that He was looking for people. Instead, He just looked around and decided to work with those who were nearby.

From what we can tell, He had little or no reason to think that those He invited to follow could ever become leaders themselves—or that they would even be good followers—but He was willing to give them a chance. Nor did it matter to Him that those who said "yes" to His invitation were generally regarded as regular guys—or worse. About the only thing Peter and Andrew could put on their résumés was "fisherman." Levi, meanwhile, was a despised tax collector. It seems the only qualification Jesus required was the willingness to make a commitment, drop whatever it was they were doing, and follow Him.

Those who want to contribute to a leadership revolution in our day have much to learn from Jesus' example. We would all do well to spend less time trying to find those who are best qualified to lead or

who show the greatest potential. For one thing, evaluating another person's potential is an inexact science, to say the least. We can't accurately predict who will or will not eventually become an effective leader—although we may think we can. Both of us have experienced the disappointment of seeing people from whom we expected great things fade into mediocrity or irrelevance. The great potential we were sure we saw in them never amounted to more than that—potential.

On the other hand, we've seen people for whom we had little or no expectation develop as leaders in ways we had never even hoped for or imagined. All who aspire to develop leaders would do well to realize that it's not up to us to decide who will or won't become a leader. To attempt to do so is to limit unfairly (and unwisely) the sacrifices people are willing to make to improve their leadership skills. It also underestimates God's power to work through those who humble themselves before Him.

ALL WHO ASPIRE TO DEVELOP LEADERS WOULD DO WELL TO REALIZE THAT IT'S NOT UP TO US TO DECIDE WHO WILL OR WON'T BECOME A LEADER.

As leaders, our better bet is to follow Jesus' example of casting a wide net by inviting as many people as possible to become part of the revolution. We don't need to do any national searches to find our future leaders—those who supposedly have the best qualifications to achieve our ministry goals. The people we need can be found among those we see every day. They attend our churches and live in our communities. As long as they are willing to serve, it doesn't really matter what potential or natural leadership ability they do or don't possess. A lack of desire cannot be fixed, coached or developed. But if people are willing—if they want to become leaders—we can welcome them with open arms and help them grow into the roles that need to be filled.

Jesus' proactive approach to leadership extended beyond His method of selecting His followers. He deliberately modeled for those

He was developing the kind of leadership He wanted them to emulate. He didn't wait for an invitation to teach, whether on a hillside or in a temple. And He didn't suggest to the moneychangers in the temple that they might want to think about the appropriateness of their activities. He overturned their tables.

In many ways, the Prince of Peace was a rabble-rouser. Countless scholars have focused on the dimension of Jesus' ministry that involved upsetting the social and political orders of the day. When Jesus appeared before Pilate, and Pilate found "no basis for a charge" (Luke 23:4) against Him, the chief priests insisted, "He stirs up the people all over Judea by his teaching. He started in Galilee and has come all the way here" (v. 5).

Because of Jesus' gentleness, kindness and compassion, we may not give much consideration to the more "Type A" dimensions of His personality. But those dimensions were there—and Jesus modeled them clearly for those He was developing, some of whom stayed with Him until the end of His earthly ministry.

## Accessible

If you've seen the movie *The Devil Wears Prada*, you'll know what we mean when we say that some leaders seem to regard aloofness and inaccessibility as part of their job description. In this film's fictional publishing company (which unfortunately represents the reality in many non-fictional organizations, including some Christian ones), the leader does not function as a servant or shepherd, but solely as "the boss." Not just any boss, either—she is likened to the devil. When the boss is in the building, everyone is on edge and uncomfortable. Everything must be perfect, or somebody will have to pay—maybe even with his or her job. It is clear to everyone at the company who is in charge of things—and who isn't.

The boss in this kind of "top down" leadership setting has virtually no connection with most of the people who are part of the organization—he or she wouldn't even recognize many of them on the street. The waiting list to get an appointment to see this leader is long. For those who are regarded as being at the bottom of the proverbial totem pole, getting such a meeting is not even possible, as several

administrative layers protect the person in charge. The thought of dropping in on him or her is unheard of.

Meanwhile, those near the top of the organizational chart are preoccupied with self-preservation. The prevailing climate is one of fear and intimidation. People don't feel free to express their viewpoints or to question "company policy." Far from considering the leader a friend or colleague, employees regard him or her with disdain. One wonders how such "leaders" are able to rise to the top of an organization. Yet somehow many do.

This kind of environment is not conducive to developing new leaders. People have little chance to grow in their leadership abilities if they never spend time with the leader or if, when they are with the leader, it's clear that the only thing important to the boss is the boss.

To be sure, the reality at many organizations—and certainly at most churches and Christian ministries—is not as severe as what we have just described. Yet when it comes to the issue of accessibility and how it affects the development of leaders, there is plenty of room for improvement and much to learn from Jesus' example. Let's take a closer look at that example now.

The Gospel record makes it unequivocally clear that the Lord made Himself completely accessible to those who followed Him. Though at times He withdrew to be alone, He spent most of His time with His disciples—teaching them, answering their questions, and frequently (as we will see in the next chapter) correcting them.

Jesus made Himself available not only to His disciples, but also to those who were not followers but needed or wanted something only the Lord could provide. On one occasion, two blind men, hoping to have their sight restored, followed Jesus when He went inside. Instead of turning them away, Jesus touched their eyes and they were healed (see Matt. 9:27-30). We read in Luke 18:35-43 that some of those accompanying Jesus to Jericho in essence told another blind man in search of sight to get away and leave Jesus alone. But "Jesus stopped and ordered the man to be brought to him" (v. 40). Then He restored his sight.

In Mark 1:35-38, we find Jesus trying to get some time alone early in the morning "while it was still dark." Peter and a few others found Him and told Him, "Everyone is looking for you!" Jesus didn't tell them

He didn't want to be bothered. Instead He suggested that they go to some nearby villages to preach, adding, "That is why I have come." Thus He defined His very purpose in terms of being accessible to people. We read later in the chapter that "Jesus could no longer enter a town openly but stayed outside in lonely places. Yet the people still came to him from everywhere" (v. 45).

JESUS DEFINED HIS VERY PURPOSE IN TERMS OF BEING ACCESSIBLE TO PEOPLE.

After the Twelve returned from a preaching and healing mission with stories to tell, they and Jesus tried to withdraw by themselves, but the crowds found out where they were and followed them (see Luke 9:1-11). Again, instead of turning them away, Jesus "welcomed them and spoke to them about the kingdom of God, and healed those who needed healing" (v. 11).

In Mark 3:20-21, we read that Jesus went into a house but "a crowd gathered, so that he and his disciples were not even able to eat. When his family heard about this, they went to take charge of him, for they said, 'He is out of his mind.' " Thus a picture emerges of Jesus being completely accessible to people—so much so that those closest to Him thought He was crazy.

Now, it's valuable for us, as leaders, to remind ourselves that as much as we want to be like Jesus, none of us is Jesus. If serving others has us skipping meals and losing sleep, it might be time to read a book or attend a seminar on the topic of self-care. It's important for ministry leaders to find balance—to take time and create space to care for ourselves and for our families. Thus, setting limits and drawing some boundaries is necessary and good. But this can be done while still embracing and following Jesus' model of accessibility.

Being accessible to people, especially those we are trying to develop as leaders, has at least as much to do with an attitude—with creating a particular atmosphere or setting the right tone—as it does with

measuring the minutes or hours we spend with them. To put it another way, a leader can spend a day or an entire weekend with others and still not be genuinely accessible to them. What's most important to those we are developing is that they know we care deeply about them and that we'll do everything in our power to be available to them if and when they need us. They want to know that there is nothing they cannot share with us, no question they should be hesitant to ask, and no topic they should be afraid to explore.

This emphasis on setting the right tone is not intended in any way to minimize the importance of actually spending time with those we are seeking to develop as leaders. Our point is simply that spending time with people will come more naturally and spontaneously if the right "atmosphere of accessibility" has been created.

WHAT'S MOST IMPORTANT TO THOSE WE ARE DEVELOPING IS THAT THEY KNOW WE CARE DEEPLY ABOUT THEM AND THAT WE'LL DO EVERYTHING IN OUR POWER TO BE AVAILABLE TO THEM.

Keep in mind that spending time with others need not always take up extra time on your schedule. Suppose, for example, that you plan to attend a conference or seminar on some aspect of ministry or church administration. Attending the event will take up a fixed amount of your time. So why not take at least one other person with you? Doing so won't eat up any more of your schedule than going to the event alone would—and as a bonus, you will almost certainly get more out of the conference if you have someone else with whom to process and reflect on the information. This might require an adjustment to the church's continuing education budget, but for those leaders who are committed to developing other leaders, this is a worthwhile habit to cultivate. Four words that we have lived by over the years—and which we believe should be at the center of the leadership revolution—are these: Never go anywhere alone!

When people have access to their leaders, the result is an environment in which everyone feels relaxed and comfortable. Despite the

existence of a clear chain of command—an organizational structure in which some people report to others—no one is given the impression that their role is any more (or less) important than anyone else's. Instead, the whole team will strive together to achieve corporate goals and vision.

This kind of environment is created in part by the ways in which people interact with one another, which is determined in large part by how the leaders interact with others in the ministry. Let's quickly consider four scenarios. In the first, people at the bottom of the organizational chart never even see the leader. In the second, people routinely pass the leader in the hallway, but he or she doesn't acknowledge them. In the third, the leader acknowledges people with a nice smile, but doesn't really know who they are. In the fourth, the leader not only smiles, but also calls people by name and perhaps even starts conversations that demonstrate that he or she knows something about what is going on in their lives. This last scenario represents the kind of servant leadership that we are convinced is most conducive to the development of leaders.

At Lawndale Community Church, it's not unusual for the church leaders to have a business meeting interrupted by someone from the congregation who stopped by to say hello or perhaps make a request or get a question answered. In some organizations, such an unexpected interruption would be problematic—possibly even grounds for dismissal. But at Lawndale, we're both encouraged and excited by the fact that this kind of thing happens regularly. It assures us that people feel that their leaders are accessible. So what if the business meeting runs a few minutes longer? That is a small price to pay for an atmosphere in which people feel comfortable approaching their leaders. (The people of Lawndale develop this comfort at an early age—not long ago, a beautiful four-year-old girl named Zariah came by my [Wayne's] house at dinnertime to give me some goldfish for my aquarium!)

This is not to say that pastors or other leaders should be completely accessible to anyone and everyone at any time. But it's one thing to have an assistant who fields phone calls and manages the daily schedule, and quite another thing to be shielded by seven or eight layers of administration or by policies and procedures that might as well be shouting, "Do not disturb." At Lawndale, we believe that creating an

atmosphere of accessibility both reflects Christ's example and is crucial to achieving our ministry goals.

## Aware (In Touch)

Jesus consistently demonstrated a high degree of awareness of what was going on around Him—of what was happening among those He was leading. This should come as no surprise, for it stands to reason that leaders who make themselves accessible to others will naturally be more in touch with what is going on in the organization or ministry, including among the so-called rank and file. Not only will the leader know if people are unhappy and grumbling about something, but he or she will also know exactly what it is the people are unhappy and grumbling about.

Among the most common complaints to be heard about leadership is that leaders are "out of touch." Let's be clear in acknowledging that both the business world and the ministry world contain chronic complainers—people who, if they can't find anything wrong, will complain about not having anything to complain about. We'll touch more on this topic later; for now our focus is on concerns that are fully or at least largely legitimate. Such concerns are raised, for example, when leaders make decisions without consulting the people who will be most affected by those decisions. When this happens, even if a particular decision happens to be correct, morale is dealt a blow.

Out-of-touch leaders generally are not aware of the issues people in the organization are dealing with, nor are they likely to recognize a downturn in morale, even a substantial one. It's quite possible, when dealing with a dysfunctional organization or ministry, to get two completely different impressions of how things are going from reading the president's report to the board on the one hand and chatting with a few randomly selected employees on the other. The gap that exists between the boardroom and the lunchroom is one way to measure the "awareness quotient" of the organization's leadership.

By contrast, let's look at some of the ways Jesus demonstrated His awareness of what was going on around Him. Mark 8:14 lets us know that one or more of the disciples had messed up by forgetting to bring bread for a planned trip in a boat. As a result, the group had just one

loaf among them. Apparently nobody wanted to tell Jesus about this oversight, although the disciples did discuss the matter among themselves (see v. 16). Verse 17, however, begins with the words, "Aware of their discussion, Jesus asked them . . ." There is no apparent reason for the Gospel writer to include these seemingly minute details—except to communicate that Jesus was completely in touch with those He was leading.

Jesus demonstrated the same kind of awareness in an interaction chronicled in John 6. Teaching in the synagogue in Capernaum, He told the people that in order to have eternal life, they would have to eat His flesh and drink His blood (see vv. 53-59). We read in verse 60: "On hearing it, many of his disciples said, 'This is a hard teaching. Who can accept it?'" Verse 61 begins very similarly to the passage discussed above: "Aware that his disciples were grumbling about this, Jesus said . . ."

THE GAP THAT EXISTS BETWEEN THE BOARDROOM AND THE LUNCHROOM IS ONE WAY TO MEASURE THE "AWARENESS QUOTIENT" OF THE ORGANIZATION'S LEADERSHIP.

Later in John's Gospel, we find yet another example of Jesus knowing what His disciples are thinking about or struggling with. In John 16:17-18, we see the disciples confused and asking themselves what Jesus had in mind when He said to them, "In a little while you will see me no more, and then after a little while you will see me." They also questioned what Jesus meant about "going to the Father," confessing, "We don't understand what he is saying."

Perhaps they felt embarrassed about not "getting it." In any case, Jesus sensed their frustration. In verse 19, we read, "Jesus saw that they wanted to ask him about this."

Because He was so aware of what was happening around Him, Jesus knew that one of those closest to Him—one of the Twelve—would deny Him, and that another would betray Him. One wonders if Judas was surprised that Jesus had figured it out, or if by then he knew Jesus

well enough to know that nothing—certainly nothing of this magnitude—ever got by Him.

The main reason Jesus was so in touch with those He was leading was that He loved them deeply. Being aware of what is going on—being in touch—is a natural attribute of loving relationships. As leaders, we demonstrate our love for those we are attempting to develop by being aware of what is going on in their lives—of the challenges they are facing and the questions they may have, including questions they find it difficult to ask.

Leaders who love those they are leading and developing do not make decisions that affect other people without giving those people an opportunity to contribute their opinions and perspectives. This approach greatly improves the chances of people respecting whatever decision is made, even if they do not agree with it. Organizational health is much improved when participants have opportunities on a regular basis to express their views, register their opinions, ask questions (even tough ones), and, if necessary, air any grievances without fear of reprisal.

AS LEADERS, WE DEMONSTRATE OUR LOVE FOR THOSE WE ARE ATTEMPTING TO DEVELOP BY BEING AWARE OF WHAT IS GOING ON IN THEIR LIVES.

The less hierarchical the organizational structure, the easier it will be for the leader to stay in touch with everyone, because the distance between leader and followers is kept to a minimum. With a non- or minimally hierarchical structure, one person doesn't tell others what to do and then walk away. Instead, team members work together. In this kind of collaborative environment, it's hard for the leader not to be aware of what's going on around him or her.

One way to create and communicate a sense of shared ministry is to provide opportunities for those leading in one area of ministry to serve under somebody else's leadership in another area. Submitting

from time to time to someone else's authority can be very helpful for leaders. Among other benefits, it keeps us humble!

Staying in touch with the people we are leading involves making a commitment to be sensitive to their wellbeing. We ask how they are doing, and not just in a perfunctory way. We find ways to demonstrate that we know what is going on in their lives. We listen carefully and notice clues—including nonverbal ones—that indicate something could be wrong.

Most fundamentally, we seek to love as Jesus loved. With love as our starting point, being proactive, accessible and aware will inevitably follow.

CHAPTER FIVE

# LEADERSHIP LESSONS FROM JESUS (PART II)

The apostle Paul wrote to the Corinthian church, "Follow my example, as I follow the example of Christ" (1 Cor. 11:1). Young people today might say more simply, "Watch and learn!" Either way, the idea is the same: We can learn a lot—and grow in our own abilities—by paying attention to the actions of people we admire and seek to emulate. In particular, those who aspire to be servant leaders benefit greatly by observing, understanding and imitating the things Jesus did as He developed a generation of leaders.

## Jesus Hung Out with People

It's easy to imagine great religious leaders of the past as being somewhat reclusive or private, perhaps even mystical or mysterious. Some might have this same impression of Jesus, given that we do read of His going off to secluded places to spend time alone with the Father (see, for example, Luke 5:16). The Gospel accounts, however, reveal a person who, far from living a cloistered life, loved to hang out with people, including regular folk. Jesus really did live out the prophecy found in Matthew 1:23: " 'They will call him Immanuel'—which means, 'God with us.' "

WE CAN LEARN A LOT—AND GROW IN OUR OWN ABILITIES—BY PAYING ATTENTION TO THE ACTIONS OF PEOPLE WE ADMIRE AND SEEK TO EMULATE.

When Jesus walked among us, He maintained a very active social life. On one occasion, He and His disciples accepted an invitation to a wedding (see John 2:1-11). We have no reason to think that the two getting married were well known or influential. They were most likely regular people. Jesus got an invitation, and He showed up. In Luke 10:38, we see Jesus accepting an invitation to enter the home of "a woman named Martha." Later, we read that "a Pharisee invited him to eat with him; so he went in and reclined at the table" (Luke 11:37). We find out in the next verse that this Pharisee took note that Jesus had not

washed His feet prior to the meal. One wonders if "reclining" in this case meant that Jesus sat back and propped His feet up on the table. In any case, it's clear He made Himself at home, dirty feet and all.

It sometimes seems like the Gospel writers go out of their way to point out that Jesus liked spending time with people whom nobody else wanted to be around. He was having dinner at Matthew's house when some of Matthew's fellow tax collectors and other "sinners" showed up to eat with Him and His disciples (see Matt. 9:10). Not surprisingly, when the Pharisees found out about this, they took Jesus to task for His unsatisfactory behavior (see v. 11). In Luke 7:36-39, we find Jesus once again having dinner at a Pharisee's house and reclining at the table. On this occasion, a local woman with a widespread reputation as a sinner came over and allowed her tears to wet Jesus' feet. After she had dried His feet with her hair and poured perfume on them, the man who had invited Jesus to dinner once again reprimanded Him.

Jesus didn't always wait to get invited to the house of some universally despised person. Zacchaeus, a chief tax collector who "wanted to see who Jesus was" but was short of stature, climbed a tree so that he could see the Lord passing through Jericho (see Luke 19:1-5). Most people wouldn't expect a religious leader to accept an invitation to have dinner with one of the most hated people in town. But what Jesus does is even more shocking than that—He invites Himself to dinner. He says, "Zacchaeus, come down immediately. I must stay at your house today" (v. 5).

One of the most compelling and revealing interactions recorded in the Gospels is John's account of Jesus' encounter with a woman at a well in Samaria (see John 4:1-26). For a Jew to associate with a Samaritan—and a woman to boot—defied all social convention. Even His disciples, who presumably knew Jesus better than anyone, were "surprised to find him talking with a woman" (v. 27).

But social convention meant nothing to Jesus. He started the conversation by asking the woman for a drink and ended up changing her life forever. The woman's testimony about her encounter with Christ then led many other Samaritans from the town to believe (see vv. 39-42). The townspeople urged Jesus to stick around for a while, and He (and presumably His disciples) ended up hanging out with their new friends for two days.

Jesus' actions as a leader cannot be separated from His influence as a developer of leaders. He allowed His followers to witness everything He did and said. Even when His behavior surprised them, He didn't back down from His principles. As a result, the disciples were transformed from thinking it inappropriate to speak with a Samaritan woman to understanding that such behavior lay at the heart of their mission.

As leaders, we have opportunities every day to model this kind of behavior for our followers—assuming we don't tuck ourselves away where no one can ever find us. Jesus did not avoid going where the regular people were. In fact, He sought out those who needed Him the most. Sometimes, as we've seen, He didn't even wait for an invitation; He invited Himself into the lives of others.

We would invite you to take a few moments right now to think about what it might look like for you to hang out with ordinary folks in your community. Maybe it means attending sporting events and school board or town council meetings. It could look like starting a conversation in a grocery store or on a street corner with someone you don't know—someone whom society might frown upon but who needs to experience the love of Jesus Christ. Imagine the effect it will have on those we seek to develop as leaders if they see us consistently demonstrating this kind of involvement in other people's lives.

## Jesus Taught at Every Opportunity

Sometimes we focus so much on Jesus' mission as the Savior of the world that we forget His role as a teacher. But Jesus seized every possible opportunity to teach. In Luke 13:22, we find Him going "through the towns and villages, teaching as he made his way to Jerusalem." After arriving in Jerusalem, Jesus taught "each day . . . at the temple" (Luke 21:37). In his Gospel, Mark describes multiple occasions on which Jesus went out by a lake and began to teach (see, for example, Mark 4:1). On one of those days, the crowd was so large that Jesus got into a boat and went out onto the lake so the people on shore could see and hear Him.

Jesus obliged when the disciples asked Him to teach them to pray (see Luke 11:1). He taught in response to questions such as, "Who is the greatest in the kingdom of heaven?" (Matt. 18:1) and "What

must I do to inherit eternal life?" (Luke 18:18). The disciples asked Jesus why they had been unable to cast out an evil spirit from a young boy (see Mark 9:28) and about signs that would signify the end of the age (see Luke 21:7), and He answered them. He even responded to questions posed by those who were out to destroy Him, such as the chief priests and teachers of the law, who said to Him, "Tell us by what authority you are doing these things. Who gave you this authority?" (Luke 20:2).

Not only did Jesus respond to people's questions, but He also sometimes posed (and answered) questions of His own. For instance, He asked His disciples, "What is the kingdom of God like? What shall I compare it to?" (Luke 13:18) and then went on to compare it to a mustard seed (v. 19) and yeast (v. 21).

JESUS TAUGHT AT ANY AND EVERY OPPORTUNITY—IN PUBLIC AND IN PRIVATE, AT THE TEMPLE, IN TOWNS AND VILLAGES, AND IN A BOAT ON A LAKE.

A picture emerges of Jesus teaching at any and every opportunity—in public and in private, at the temple, in towns and villages, and in a boat on a lake. But the best example of Jesus' influence as a teacher might well be His historic "Sermon on the Mount" (found in Matt. 5:3–7:27). Those whose Bibles use red letters to signify the words of Christ will find several columns of nothing but red in this passage, whose content has inspired countless sermons over the years. This sermon is where Jesus gives us the Beatitudes (5:3-12). He also likens His followers to salt and light (5:13-16), redefines murder and adultery (5:21-30), tells us to love our enemies (5:43-48) and to give to the needy (6:1-4), gives us the Lord's Prayer (6:9-13), presents a pure approach to fasting (6:16-18), challenges us to store up treasures in heaven (6:19-24), urges us not to worry (6:25-34), warns us not to judge others (7:1-5), and instructs us through metaphors featuring

doors (7:7-8), wide and narrow gates (7:13-14), and wise and foolish builders (7:24-27). All in one sermon!

Note that Matthew introduces this amazing sermon with the words "and he began to teach them" (Matt. 5:2). For Jesus, this sermon was all about teaching. Matthew also notes that as the crowds gathered on the mountainside, "his disciples came to him" (Matt. 5:1), giving the impression that those closest to Christ—those He was most intentionally developing as leaders—had front row seats.

If our desire is to develop leaders the way Jesus did, we will make a similar commitment to teaching, in both formal and informal settings. Everywhere we go and in everything we do, we will be aware of the teaching opportunities we have. Every sermon we preach and every lecture we deliver is an opportunity to teach. Every field trip or missions trip we take with the youth group—including those long hours we spend in the car, van or bus—provides teaching opportunities. Every visit to a Sunday School class, a Bible club or a ministry program gives us another chance to teach—whether we are asked to present a full lesson or simply say a few words.

IF OUR DESIRE IS TO DEVELOP LEADERS THE WAY JESUS DID, WE WILL MAKE A SIMILAR COMMITMENT TO TEACHING, IN BOTH FORMAL AND INFORMAL SETTINGS.

As we seize these opportunities to teach, we can use them to pursue the goal of developing leaders for the revolution. I (Wayne) have preached whole sermons whose sole purpose was to help people recognize their potential as leaders (you'll see an example of this in chapter 13). Sunday School classes can focus on leadership skills for Christian ministry. The perspectives and skills that go into being an effective leader are not numerous, but they do need to be presented clearly and frequently, so that people have opportunities to adopt and cultivate them. The more people are taught the funda-

mentals of leadership, the more they will grow in both their ability and their confidence to lead.

## Jesus Was Authentic—He Showed His Vulnerability

The fact that Jesus lived a sinless life and is a member of the Holy Trinity can result in the downplaying of His humanity. However, traditional orthodox doctrine holds that He was at once both fully God and fully human. He was sinless, but He was not invulnerable. In fact, He was susceptible to pain and sickness, and to the same human emotions all of us feel and with which all of us struggle. If He stubbed His toe on a rock, it hurt. If someone died or let Him down in some way, it made Him sad. His humanity was completely authentic.

It's important to note that Jesus made no attempt to stoically hide His pain or His emotions. In fact, He openly displayed His human vulnerability and His authenticity by expressing feelings of sadness, fear and anger. Matthew records Jesus' grief at receiving the news of John the Baptist's death (see Matt. 14:13), and John tells us that Jesus wept over the death of Lazarus (see John 11:35). What's interesting about this is that Jesus wept even though He was about to raise Lazarus from the dead. It could be that in His weeping, He was identifying with the pain of Lazarus's sister and others whose grieving caused Jesus to be "deeply moved in spirit and troubled" (John 11:33). He was again "troubled in spirit" prior to His painful announcement that one of those He had chosen to be closer to Him than all others was going to betray Him (see John 13:21).

Jesus showed that He was capable of fierce anger by overturning the tables and benches of moneychangers intent on converting a house of prayer into what Jesus called "a den of robbers" (see Mark 11:15-17).

As the end drew near, and Jesus' immediate future came into clearer focus, He faced it not without emotion but with overwhelming dread. In the Garden of Gethsemane, He confessed to the three He had brought with Him, "My soul is overwhelmed with sorrow to the point of death" (Mark 14:34). Praying on the Mount of Olives, He begged His Father not to go through with the plan, though He ended His petition by saying, "Not my will, but yours be done" (Luke 22:42).

In anguish and praying even more earnestly, "His sweat was like drops of blood falling to the ground" (v. 44).

Those of us who are leaders and developers of leaders have much to learn from Jesus' example of unashamedly putting His human vulnerability on display for all to see. Showing vulnerability is an act of humility. It helps people to identify with their leaders by communicating that leaders are not very different—if they are different at all—from others. They are not immune to sadness, fear or anger.

Authenticity and transparency are important attributes of servant leaders. Leaders who are not servant leaders don't allow people to see them as they truly are—pros and cons, strengths and weakness, warts and all. They never want others to see them sad, upset or discouraged. They become aloof. They build walls—walls that might not limit physical access, but that clearly and consistently limit emotional access.

LEADERS WHO ARE NOT SERVANT LEADERS DON'T ALLOW PEOPLE TO SEE THEM AS THEY TRULY ARE—PROS AND CONS, STRENGTHS AND WEAKNESS, WARTS AND ALL.

It can be challenging for leaders—especially male leaders—to get beyond the notion that people should never see us cry. But authentic leaders have no use for plastic smiles or for maintaining that stiff upper lip. Not only is it good for us to cry, but it is also sometimes appropriate for us to cry publicly. I (Wayne) cried on more than one occasion when sharing with the congregation about my mother's progression through Alzheimer's disease. For me not to have cried would have been inauthentic. I cried before the congregation again on the Sunday after learning that a close friend (he had been the best man at my wedding) had taken his own life. Not to cry would have been dishonest. It would also have limited my ability to get a message of hope through to someone who might be contemplating suicide.

Just a few weeks prior to the time of this writing, I preached a sermon based on the eighth chapter of Zechariah. Verses 4 and 5 paint

a picture of elderly men and women sitting in the streets of Jerusalem, each of them with a cane in hand. Those same streets are "filled with boys and girls playing there." I could not help but contrast the streets of this peaceful scene with the streets of Chicago, where during the first few months of the year murders were up by 100 percent over the previous year. During the first service, I was so overcome by emotion at this comparison that I erupted in tears. It took awhile for me to compose myself.

During the Sunday School hour, Anne asked me if I would be okay doing the sermon in the second service, and I assured her I would be. But when I got to the same point in the sermon, I again started to weep uncontrollably. If anything, it was worse. Or was it better? When teenagers are being killed on our streets, shouldn't we weep over the pain and tragedy of it? As a pastor, by sharing my emotions with the congregation, I was able to help people deliberate on this epidemic of violence more than they might have otherwise.

Now, let's be clear that what we're talking about here is the expression of genuine emotions—not the shedding of tears to put on a show. In that case, crying is manipulative and inauthentic. Servant leaders and their followers will know in their hearts the difference between real and fake.

Another way we show our authenticity is by being open about the challenges we face in our personal and family lives. When Anne and I have struggled with one thing or another, we've shared our struggles with other church leaders—not only because we need their support and advice, but also because we want to identify with all who struggle, and to enable them to identify with us.

As for anger, some occasions call for leaders who are developing others to get upset and express anger. Sometimes that's exactly what those we are developing need from us. Anyone who has coached a sports team knows that some players are motivated by a supportive pat on the back, while others do better if they receive a good, swift kick in the butt every once in a while. (We're speaking figuratively here—we certainly are not suggesting that anger should be expressed through violent means under any circumstances!) Common sense and the counsel of others will generally make it clear if someone has a problem controlling anger. Discernment is always required, but when

expressed appropriately and at the right time, anger can be a powerful tool for correcting self-destructive or otherwise harmful behaviors, and for motivating those we lead to strive for excellence.

Even before Jesus' birth, the scriptural precedent for being real before God and before others had been established. Many of the psalms, for example, begin as pleas for help and acknowledgments of distress or even doubt. For instance, David cried out in Psalm 55, "Listen to my prayer, O God, do not ignore my plea; hear me and answer me. My thoughts trouble me and I am distraught. . . . My heart is in anguish within me" (vv. 1-4). Then there are the words Jesus quoted while hanging on the cross: "My God, my God, why have you forsaken me?" (Ps. 22:1).

Don't be afraid to express your emotions—to be real. Every time you do so, you are in some way modeling servant leadership and, perhaps without being aware of it, shaping someone who wants to lead as you lead.

## Jesus Prepared People to Follow Him

In many ways, the role of a leader is similar to that of a coach, whose job it is to prepare his players adequately in order to give them the best chance to win. There is perhaps no worse feeling for a coach than the feeling that he's failed to prepare his team, especially when his players go out and get embarrassed.

Matthew 10:5-42 contains the final instructions Jesus gave the Twelve before sending them out on a mission to announce the coming of the Kingdom. The passage brings to mind a coach's pre-game speech—albeit a rather long one. Jesus told His team of disciples where to go, what to preach, what to do, where to stay, whom to watch out for, and much more. (Mark records that Jesus also instructed the apostles on what to take with them and what to wear [Mark 6:8-9].) Before sending the apostles into the game, as it were, Jesus "gave them authority to drive out evil spirits and to heal every disease and sickness" (Matt. 10:2). In other words, through both teaching and equipping, He prepared them for what lay ahead.

As developers of leaders, we have the responsibility to make sure those we "send out" are adequately prepared—that they are capable

of carrying out whatever assignments they accept, and that they have the support they need to succeed. This is especially true for those who are lacking in confidence and self-esteem, for whom even a minor failure in the beginning could result in a major setback in their development.

## Jesus Gave People Assignments

Once His followers were prepared and ready for some game action, Jesus didn't allow them to sit on the sidelines. He gave them important things to do. Certainly, the mission mentioned above—on which, according to Luke, the disciples were "to preach the kingdom of God and to heal the sick" (Luke 9:2)—is a prime example of Jesus entrusting meaningful work to His followers.

That mission was not an isolated event; it was part of a pattern of Jesus assigning tasks to those He was developing—and providing them with the resources and authority they needed to carry out those tasks. In Mark's account of the feeding of the 5,000, we find Jesus directing His disciples with regard to seating arrangements for the masses (see Mark 6:39). They also get the assignment of delivering the loaves and fishes (see v. 41). In Luke 22:8, Jesus assigns Peter and John to "go and make preparations for us to eat the Passover"—the meal we now know as the Last Supper. The Lord knew how to delegate; He kept His followers busy, and not just with busywork. He invited them to participate in His ministry in significant ways.

AS DEVELOPERS OF LEADERS, WE HAVE THE RESPONSIBILITY TO MAKE SURE THOSE WE "SEND OUT" ARE ADEQUATELY PREPARED.

Of course, the most far-reaching and ambitious assignment He gave to the 11 remaining apostles is recorded in Matthew 28:19-20: "Therefore go and make disciples of all nations, baptizing them in the name of the Father and of the Son and of the Holy Spirit, and teaching

them to obey everything I have commanded you." This is still the Church's assignment today, and developing servant leaders is an important part of carrying out this commission.

If we as leaders and developers of leaders have prepared people well, they will be looking for things to do. Very few things are more frustrating than being totally prepared to do something and then not having the chance to do it. Athletes who are in top physical condition, who know all the plays, and who have studied the game plan despise having to sit on the bench. Musicians who have spent months practicing for a concert are crushed if it snows so much that the event has to be cancelled. Most people in work environments prefer having a little too much to do to having nothing to do all day.

The assignments we give people should be important and challenging—tasks that will help them grow and give them opportunities to lead. Ideally, we should have some assignments in mind as we are preparing people.

THE ASSIGNMENTS WE GIVE PEOPLE SHOULD BE IMPORTANT AND CHALLENGING—TASKS THAT WILL HELP THEM GROW AND GIVE THEM OPPORTUNITIES TO LEAD.

A key to succeeding at leadership development is avoiding the temptation to micromanage. Give people space to do things their way, even if their way is different from your way. Don't move in and take over to make sure the job gets done right. Getting the job done perfectly is not as important as giving people the chance to learn.

Think about a time when you asked some techie to teach you how to do something on your computer. You probably made it clear that you wanted to do the work, and that his (or her) job was simply to tell you what to do. But techies are notorious for getting frustrated by computer illiterates. You moved too slowly, and your teacher started doing things for you—and before you knew it, he or she had taken over completely. Now, whatever it was you wanted to get done got done. But you didn't learn a thing. Let's not be impatient techies who

get stuff done but make it hard for those we are developing to learn new skills!

At Lawndale Community Church, it's not difficult to find ways for people to lead, given that there are so many needs in the community. Leading the effort to secure toys at Christmas for children who might not otherwise get them is one of many examples. Another great opportunity for shared leadership came up recently, when we decided to hold a movie night at church for the men of the congregation. Some volunteers made arrangements to get the movie and the equipment needed to show it. Others volunteered to set up. Some took care of the food, while others agreed to lead the discussion afterwards. In all, about 150 men came to see the movie, and nearly half that number played a part in making the event happen.

An important thing to keep in mind as you are delegating leadership tasks is that sometimes people will fail. Jesus' disciples were no exception. Mark records that the disciples were once unable to cast an evil spirit from a boy (see Mark 9:18). They later asked Jesus why they couldn't do it (see v. 28), and, like a good developer of leaders, He told them (see v. 29). People learn by doing—and they learn a lot by failing. So keep giving meaningful and significant assignments, along with the freedom to come up short. Such freedom brings with it rich opportunities for learning and growth.

## Jesus Defended His Followers

The Gospels document more than one occasion on which Jesus came to the defense of those with whom He was closest. In Matthew 12:1-8, we see Him defending His disciples against the Pharisees, who criticized them for picking grain on the Sabbath in order to satisfy their hunger. According to Matthew 15:1-9, when the Pharisees again found fault with the disciples (this time for not washing their hands before eating), Jesus called them hypocrites for breaking the command of God for the sake of their tradition. In Luke 19:37-39, we read that some Pharisees called for Jesus to rebuke His disciples for referring to Him as the king. Jesus responded by saying that if the disciples remained quiet, the stones would cry out (see v. 40). In John 14:1, we find Jesus comforting His disciples: "Do not let your hearts be troubled."

Similarly, there will be times when those we are developing will need us to comfort and defend them. The more they accept positions of leadership, the more they open themselves to criticism. This is not to say that we should allow mistakes or moral failures to go uncorrected. But even those who have failed, in order to learn from their mistakes, need someone to come to their defense.

This advice is especially relevant for those who are ministering in places like North Lawndale, where many of those we are attempting to develop struggle with addictions or get caught up in various kinds of criminal behavior. More than once, a delegation from Lawndale Community Church has shown up in court to demonstrate support for someone who has been falsely accused or, if guilty of the charge, is in need of assistance to make the most of a second, third or fourth chance.

Whether or not you are working in a community that faces these particular challenges, keep in mind that your developing leaders make themselves vulnerable to critique and discouragement whenever they step into an unfamiliar or challenging new role. They are much more likely to flourish if they know that someone is in their corner.

## Jesus Demonstrated Honesty and Candor

As much as Jesus defended His disciples, He also criticized them when they deserved it. He didn't pull many punches. He let them know when they messed up. He was forthright, honest and candid with those He was leading and developing. Often, Jesus' love for His followers was a tough kind of love. If you read through the Gospels with a particular focus on how often Jesus rebukes His disciples for one reason or another, you might be surprised at the frequency of the critiques. On one occasion, almost immediately following Jesus' spirited defense of His disciples to a group of Pharisees, the disciples asked Him to explain the parable He had just told. Jesus' first response was, "Are you still so dull?" (Matt. 15:16). Another time, after telling them they lacked faith, Jesus again criticized the disciples, essentially for being lame-brained—for not understanding His metaphor regarding the yeast of the Pharisees (see Matt. 16:8-11).

After Peter challenged Jesus' statement that He would suffer and be killed (see Matt. 16:21-22), Jesus responded, "Get behind me, Satan!

You are a stumbling block to me; you do not have in mind the things of God, but the things of men" (v. 23). Jesus rebuked apostles James and John for wanting to call fire down from heaven to destroy an inhospitable Samaritan village (see Luke 9:52-55). He also chastised His disciples for rebuking those who wanted to bring children to Jesus so He could touch them (see Mark 10:13-14). As Mark puts it, "when Jesus saw this, he was indignant" (v. 14).

THE OPENNESS, HONESTY AND FORTHRIGHTNESS JESUS PRACTICED WITH HIS DISCIPLES CHARACTERIZED HIS APPROACH TO THE REST OF LIFE AS WELL.

In Luke 10:41, we see Jesus correcting Martha, who had criticized her sister, Mary, for spending time listening to Jesus' teaching instead of helping with the housework. He criticized His disciples for being indignant over a woman who poured some expensive perfume on His head (see Matt. 26:6-13). Less than a week later, He rebuked one of His followers for using a sword to cut off the ear of a high priest's servant (see vv. 51-52).

The openness, honesty and forthrightness Jesus practiced with His disciples characterized His approach to the rest of life as well. When questioned by a high priest about His teaching (see John 18:19), Jesus replied, "I have spoken openly to the world. I always taught in synagogues or at the temple, where all the Jews come together. I said nothing in secret" (v. 20).

Unfortunately, honesty and candor are not always considered strengths of the contemporary Church. Today, when someone says or does something wrong, many prefer not to address it—the more politically correct approach seems to be to let things slide. It's reasonable to conclude that, in a time when people are looking for meaning in life, this lack of candor is a major contributing factor to our country's well-documented decline in church membership and attendance. It may well be that too many churches are simply going through the motions. The sermons aren't very challenging because

the pastor is fearful of offending someone. The "religious stuff" that takes place on Sunday mornings doesn't have much relevance for the rest of the week. People nod on their way out and say, "Nice service," but church is more theater than training ground—and sometimes not even very good theater.

In this kind of church culture, few if any lives are changed in a substantive way. People avoid talking about real life issues or about revolutionizing their communities for Christ. They are afraid to be too candid for fear that some in the church will take offense and leave. What we may fail to consider is the possibility that keeping everything on such a surface level could be the reason some people are leaving—or not coming to church in the first place.

If people are going to improve, they need to know the truth about themselves, even if—perhaps especially if—the truth is not easy to hear. They need to hear it in sermons and in small-group meetings, as well as from individuals—especially their leaders—whom they respect and whose judgment they trust.

IF PEOPLE ARE GOING TO IMPROVE, THEY NEED TO KNOW THE TRUTH ABOUT THEMSELVES, EVEN IF THE TRUTH IS NOT EASY TO HEAR.

We are both blessed to have married women who from the beginning modeled and practiced honesty and candor in areas big and small. Both Vera Mae Perkins and Anne Gordon subscribe to the belief that a true friend is someone who is brave enough to tell you what you most need (but might not want) to hear. Vera Mae has no trouble telling me (John) to watch out for the bits of gunk that sometimes get stuck at the corners of my mouth when I'm speaking or preaching. And more than once over the years, she's let me know that she thought my successes had made me a little too big for my britches.

When I (Wayne) truly want to know whether one of my sermons hit or missed the mark, the person I trust the most to tell me the truth

is Anne. I still remember when Anne and I were dating, and she got mad about something I did and gave me what I now call the "and another thing" speech. She started out with one thing and ended up telling me about 10 things (she says it was only 3 or 4) I was doing wrong. At first I wondered if this relationship would work, since I had a natural preference for someone who would worship the ground I walked on. But I quickly came to realize that the best chance I had to improve as a person and as a leader was to choose a life partner who could not separate her love for me from her honesty with me. When it comes to developing leaders, Anne has not been just a support person, but she has also been a fully engaged partner.

As developers of leaders, when it comes to helping people improve their leadership skills, it is our responsibility to be especially candid and forthright. If someone preaches in church or does a children's sermon or reads the Scripture lesson, our role is to sit with them afterwards and tell them what they did well and where there is room for improvement. When a particular project for which they were responsible is completed (or even if it's ongoing), we have an opportunity to provide an honest appraisal of their work that will help them do even better in future endeavors. By the way, this critiquing should be reciprocal; servant leaders will be open to receiving the feedback—both positive and negative—of others.

Some who are trying to improve their skills will welcome even your negative comments and will thank you for them. For those with fragile egos, a negative critique can be harder to take. It's important to make sure that these persons feel affirmed for their efforts and for their progress, even when there is still plenty of room for growth. One of our associate pastors at Lawndale seems to have a special ability to present a negative critique in such a way that people are thankful for his words. But whether or not we are particularly gifted in this area, all leaders can work to develop this important leadership skill.

Churches and leaders that choose to cultivate openness and honesty can count on a certain degree of conflict; it comes with this territory and is an inevitable result of keeping issues and problems out in the open instead of trying to ignore or suppress them. The fact is, conflict has a way of rising to the surface eventually. So it's better to address any problems in the church or ministry honestly, openly,

quickly and—unless there are issues of personal privacy involved—publicly. If doing so leads to conflict, the community's job is to get it completely out in the open, address it, and then get over it.

This approach might seem a little daunting in church or ministry settings that are not used to conflict and that don't have a tradition of openness and honesty. That's why it's important for leaders to create an environment in which honesty is the norm, not the exception. It's probably best for this to take place gradually, not all of a sudden. Leaders set the tone for such an environment, and a good first step is for them to be open to acknowledging their own mistakes and shortcomings in a sincere way. Both of us have fumbled the ball many times and have thrown a lot of interceptions. If you can identify with this, you're not alone. So don't be afraid to talk about your shortcomings. Let people know that you know you are far from perfect. Invite people to critique you. Make it clear to everyone that it's okay to find fault with others so long as we do it with a loving spirit and in a supportive way. That's how we all get better.

## Jesus Never Gave Up on People

Jesus believed in second chances—and third and fourth and . . . Apparently recognizing how challenging life and growth can be for some, He never gave up on anybody. When Peter asked Jesus how many times he should forgive a brother who sinned against him, Jesus replied, "I tell you, not up to seven times, but seventy times seven!" (Matt. 18:22, *AMP*). In other words, never give up on that person.

Jesus communicated to the Samaritan woman at the well, to Zacchaeus, and to many others that they could start over again. But it was Peter, the very one who wanted to know when he could stop granting second chances to a brother or sister, who took the top spot on the list of people He never gave up on. Jesus both praised and rebuked Peter on numerous occasions. When Peter (called Simon at the time) was the first to recognize Jesus as the long-awaited Messiah, the Lord told him that from that point on, he would be known as Peter, the rock on which the Lord's Church would be built (see Matt. 16:16-18). It's quite possible that Peter wasn't even sure at that point what Jesus was talking about—but he certainly must have felt affirmed.

Yet it was Peter who, even after Jesus told him he would do it, denied Christ three times, choosing personal security over truth and righteousness (see Matt. 26:69-75). This was a terrible failing, but Jesus did not give up on Peter. After the Resurrection, He created an opportunity for Peter to tell Him three times—one for each denial—that he loved Him (see John 21:15-17). As the book of Acts attests, Peter took full advantage of this second chance. Just as Jesus had predicted, he became the rock of the Early Church—an uncompromising witness for Christ and a great leader.

JESUS RECOGNIZED HOW CHALLENGING LIFE AND GROWTH CAN BE FOR SOME, AND HE NEVER GAVE UP ON ANYBODY.

Jesus didn't give up on Thomas, either. Thomas at first doubted that Jesus had risen from the dead as He said He would, but Jesus didn't write him off. Instead, He invited Thomas to touch His wounds so that Thomas, like the others, could proclaim, "My Lord and my God!" (John 21:24-28). Although some have a negative impression of "Doubting Thomas," there is no reason to believe that the resurrected Christ approached him in anything other than a kind, nonjudgmental, loving way.

If churches gave up on every person who came up short, there would soon be no one left in the pews. We see this especially clearly at Lawndale. The story of our ministry is the story of people who have been broken and are constantly fighting back. More than half of our staff members have been to prison at least once (and not as visitors). Not long ago, we hired a man to work in our health center who had just gotten clean from drugs—for at least the seventh time. Once a man who was working for our Hope Fencing business stole the truck and a bunch of tools so he could sell them for drugs—that's how powerful his urge to use was. But two years later, he was back working in another of our businesses.

When is it time to finally stop giving chances? Our answer is: when people stop wanting them. It's just that simple. Does that mean that sometimes we as leaders will get "used"? Absolutely. That's the risk that comes with giving people more chances. Think about Jesus' treatment of Peter. He knew Peter would deny Him three times. Not exactly a model of loyalty. Yet Jesus kept him "on staff."

WHEN IS IT TIME TO FINALLY STOP GIVING CHANCES? WHEN PEOPLE STOP WANTING THEM. IT'S JUST THAT SIMPLE.

This is not to say that we allow people to get or do anything and everything they want. We have no interest in enabling illegal and destructive behavior. We do not hesitate to fire people from their jobs or pull them from church leadership as a result of something they have done. We take church discipline very seriously. When people break the law or engage in behavior that is offensive or dangerous to others or to themselves, there are consequences. That doesn't mean we don't still love them or won't give them another chance—especially since we recognize the world's hesitance to hire people with criminal records, making Lawndale one of the few places where people are able to get that next chance.

But there are prerequisites for returning to work or leadership. First, people must demonstrate that they are repentant—that they are genuinely sorry for what they have done and sincerely committed to making a change of direction in their lives. Ministry leaders working collaboratively can usually agree if the repentance is sincere. Second, they must be willing to pay the price for what they've done. Perhaps they will not be permitted to hold a position of leadership for at least a year, or they may have to start at a lower-level job and work their way back up. Each situation is different.

With consequences involved, some will stay and some will flee. Those who flee usually aren't truly sorry or ready to make a change. But

when they are repentant, and when they do come back, we welcome them with open arms. We want people to know that we will always be a place they are free to return to. Jesus didn't give up on people. With His help, neither do we.

CHAPTER SIX

# THE CRITICAL ROLE OF MODELING

I (John) have on many occasions been surprised to learn how closely other people have been observing me, my family and our ministry. When Vera Mae and I moved to Pasadena in 1982, we settled in an area that had the highest daytime crime rate in Southern California. Drug dealers had taken over our block; they sold drugs right out in the open. Our house was firebombed as a result of our efforts to work with the police to shut down the drug traffic.

Undercover law enforcement officials occupied our house for the better part of a week so that they could take pictures and gather evidence in order to make arrests. One of the men who got arrested eventually asked Vera Mae to take care of the children he was leaving behind. We went to court to try to get custody, but the judge chose to have the children live with their aunt, whom we tried to support for the next several months. I've never forgotten how closely this man was watching us—and apparently respecting (if not admiring) what we were doing, even though we were in some ways his enemy.

In her book, *Hungry Ghosts*, Mary Taylor Previte, the great-granddaughter of missionary pioneer Hudson Taylor, provides another telling illustration of the power of modeling. When she was 14 years old, Mary lost her left hand as the result of an accident with a buzz saw. Despite the challenges, she didn't let her injury stop her from doing anything she otherwise would have done. She learned to do everything—tie her shoes, cook, type, and much more—with one hand.

Many years after her accident, Mary had an eye-opening experience with her young child:

> Alice, my daughter, taught me a lesson one day. She was three years old, standing in a green corduroy jumper on a kitchen chair, helping grind carrots for a carrot cake.
>
> I watched . . . a child who had grown up with a mother with one hand. . .
>
> I handed her an egg, to let her break it into the bowl. A child of three.
>
> I saw her take the egg and break it open—with one hand.[1]

The concept and practice of modeling is what unites the two topics we have been discussing—leadership and leadership development.

Although these topics are distinct, there is a sense in which they cannot be separated from each other, because even if a leader did nothing intentionally to develop other leaders—offered no programs or direct advice—that leader would still be developing other leaders based solely on the fact that he or she was being observed.

As human beings, one of the primary ways we learn is by observing—by seeing how something is done and then imitating what we have seen. What we have observed might not be the best way or the easiest way, as was the case with Mary Previte's daughter. But often it's the only way we know.

AS HUMAN BEINGS, ONE OF THE PRIMARY WAYS WE LEARN IS BY OBSERVING—BY SEEING HOW SOMETHING IS DONE AND THEN IMITATING WHAT WE HAVE SEEN.

People—especially young people—make a special effort to copy those whom they respect or admire. In playgrounds and Little League fields all over the country, kids imitate the batting stance or swing of their favorite baseball player. Anyone who has seen footage of professional basketball games prior to the mid-1980s knows how the uniform styles have changed. Back in the day, players' "shorts" really were short. But then Michael Jordan came along and decided he had a preference for longer shorts. To this day, his style is modeled at all levels, from children's leagues to high school to college to the pros. Everyone wanted to "be like Mike."

The business and education worlds understand the importance of modeling. Many undergraduate and graduate programs partner with businesses to provide an opportunity called "shadowing" to their students. In this type of internship, the student follows a professional around—acting as his or her "shadow" for a few hours each week—to see how a job is done. The intern might or might not have the opportunity to ask questions. If so, it's an added bonus. But the main point of the exercise is to observe.

One of the things we need to understand about modeling is that we don't have a choice about whether or not to do it. We can't stop other people from watching us or from being influenced by our behavior. We sometimes hear professional athletes who are not the best at setting a good example proclaim that they never wanted to be role models and that being a positive example is not part of their job description. Both of these statements are true, but the fact is they are role models whether they like it or not. They don't have a choice about that. The only choice they have is whether to be a good role model, a bad one, or something in between.

WE CAN'T STOP OTHER PEOPLE FROM WATCHING US OR FROM BEING INFLUENCED BY OUR BEHAVIOR.

This same choice confronts all of us who are parents and grandparents, aunts and uncles, teachers and preachers, leaders of ministries, neighbors and friends. As long as someone is watching, we are modeling something—and often those who are observing us are watching a lot more closely than we think. Again, our influence, whether intended or unintended, is especially great among those who are young and impressionable. Thus it is incumbent on all of us to be keenly and constantly aware of our powerful roles as models.

## Undoing Previous Damage

Those of us who intentionally seek to develop young leaders face a challenge that goes far beyond people not having access to good role models. Sadly, the models that many children and youth have been observing (whether in person or through the media) and from whom they've been learning have set overwhelmingly bad examples. Thus, "undoing" can be just as important as doing.

No one knows this better than Mary Previte, who has worked for two decades as the top administrator at the Camden (New Jersey) County

Youth Center, in essence a juvenile prison for violent offenders. Providing insight into the youth she has tried to help, she writes:

> In my small and quiet suburb, I always feel safe. I want to assume that everybody does. These children don't. I see children from the war zone of the city, "shell-shocked" like veterans of wartime combat, wounded spirits unable to shake off depression, unable to make new lives. I see it in teenagers whose shock regresses them to their childhood—grown bodies unconsciously reaching for the safety of a womb—teenagers sucking their thumbs, wetting their beds, sometimes refusing to speak. I see it in teenagers attacking an unsafe world. Victims becoming the victimizers. Why are we surprised? Why? Children mirror the worst behavior in adult models.[2]

In one of her book's saddest anecdotes, Previte tells the story of how excited the youth in the detention center got over the idea of putting together a special Parents' Night for their moms and dads. Working together with administrators, the boys and girls had hopes of connecting with their parents, perhaps showing them that they'd made progress—that they'd turned a corner. Previte writes:

> A committee of the youngsters joined in mailing the invitations. One team spruced up the classroom. Another set out cookies and juice. Another coached student hosts and hostesses on how to be the welcoming committee. When Parents' Night arrived, at 7:00 P.M. the boys kept watching for headlights in the parking lot. And again at 7:30. By eight o'clock we knew. No one was coming. We could change our world inside the Youth Center. But not the outside world.[3]

This story reminds us of the oft-repeated African proverb: "It takes a village to raise a child." Two parents—even two responsible parents—were never enough. Still, having involved parents gives young people a great advantage. When parents are absent—or when they are setting a bad example—the village has to play an even bigger role to help the children grow and develop in healthy ways. American culture, however,

has to a large extent lost sight of the concept of village—of community. By and large, children in previous generations had to answer to more than just their own parents. If neighbors or teachers became aware of a child's academic struggles or wayward behavior, they made sure to address it in one way or another—at the very least, by making sure the parents knew about it.

My (Wayne's) three children and their values have been shaped to a huge extent by the people of Lawndale, especially of Lawndale Community Church, and by John, who has been like a third grandfather to them. They had a village at their disposal. In contrast, many children and youth have neither a village nor parents who model the attitudes and behaviors they will need to develop in order to become all that God intends for them to be. The challenge is especially great in the context of the permanent underclass, but let's not make the mistake of assuming that this reality is confined to dilapidated urban areas. It's true in much of rural and suburban culture as well—too many children have lost one or both of their parents, or have parents who are not engaged in their lives in any meaningful way.

IF WE ARE TO SUPPLY THE MODELING THAT YOUNG PEOPLE NEED, IT'S IMPORTANT FOR THE CHURCH TO BECOME THE VILLAGE—THE COMMUNITY—FOR THOSE WHO LACK POSITIVE ROLE MODELS IN THEIR LIVES.

If we are to supply the modeling that young people need, it's important for the Church to become the village—the community—for those who lack positive role models in their lives. Many people in church congregations, as part of welcoming new members, take vows to do all in their power to contribute to the spiritual growth and development of those they are welcoming. It is vital that the Church as a whole commit to making sure these are not just empty words. At Lawndale, it's common practice for people to work in pairs, so that one person can model for another how to do a particular ministry task or fill a specific role in the congregation. Our informal motto, "Never

go anywhere alone," has served us well. Also key, of course, is finding ways to reach those who are not part of our fellowships but who are in desperate need of positive influences in their lives.

PEOPLE WHO ARE EXPOSED TO POSITIVE MODELS HAVE A CHANCE TO OVERCOME THE PAIN AND DEFICIENCIES OF THEIR PASTS AND BUILD A MORE FULFILLING FUTURE.

People who are exposed to positive models have a chance to overcome the pain and deficiencies of their pasts and to build a more fulfilling future, including a future as leaders. Often such persons become the most inspiring role models for others, because they are living proof that it is possible to rise above the challenges of a negative past.

## Modeling and Leadership Development

We cannot overstate the importance of modeling servant leadership for those whom we are seeking to train as leaders. Giving people the chance to witness firsthand what servant leaders do will go a long way toward providing them with effective leadership principles and skills. Bestselling author Donald Phillips, in his introduction to *Martin Luther King, Jr. on Leadership*, put it this way:

> So how do we learn to be effective leaders? We learn by observing successful individuals; by studying those who have demonstrated their abilities with tangible, visceral results. When studying great leaders of the past, consistent patterns begin to emerge; common skills become readily apparent; and certain personal traits appear and reappear time after time—from leader to leader, from century to century.[4]

People learn to lead not only by studying the philosophies of famous or successful leaders, but also by observing the day-to-day actions of those leaders. As we have seen, Jesus' efforts to develop leaders

went far beyond increasing their spiritual wisdom. He also offered considerable guidance—both through His words and through His actions—on the "nuts and bolts" skills that are of value to leaders.

As noted earlier, this begins with spending time with those we are developing and continues through targeted instruction. Many times, these two priorities can be combined. When you have a speaking engagement somewhere, you can take someone along with you so they can see how you handle yourself in various situations. Are you teaching a Sunday School class? Invite someone to co-teach it with you. Give him or her a chance to lead the class occasionally, and afterwards discuss what went well and what could have gone better. Do the same with business meetings and other activities. Let people see you make mistakes. If they don't notice your mistakes, point them out and explain that you are still growing, learning and seeking to improve as a leader—just like they are.

PEOPLE LEARN TO LEAD NOT ONLY BY STUDYING THE PHILOSOPHIES OF FAMOUS OR SUCCESSFUL LEADERS, BUT ALSO BY OBSERVING THE DAY-TO-DAY ACTIONS OF THOSE LEADERS.

For some of us, it's unpleasant to think about the fact that we will not be in our positions of leadership forever, but that's the truth. In fact, there are no guarantees that any of us will be around a month or even a week from now. When you are no longer leading your church, ministry or other organization, who will take your place? Has that person been sufficiently prepared? Will that person be ready to carry on without losing any ground?

In sum, as you model leadership, make sure that other people are watching you as often as possible. Create opportunities for those you are developing to see you in action. Be patient with them, recognizing that everyone comes from a different starting point, and some have a lot of ground to cover in terms of their social and intellectual development. Point out to them things they should be noticing. Affirm their

growth, and tell them about areas where there is room for further growth. Teach them the importance of modeling for others what you have modeled for them. With each encounter, consider how deeply you care about your ministry and how much you want it to thrive long after you are gone. Recognize that those you are developing will be the ones to whom you hand the baton to continue the race in the name of Christ and in pursuit of the kingdom of God.

**Notes**

1. Mary Taylor Previte, *Hungry Ghosts* (Grand Rapids, MI: Zondervan, 1994), pp. 267-268.
2. Ibid., p. 202.
3. Ibid., pp. 49-50.
4. Donald T. Phillips, *Martin Luther King, Jr. on Leadership* (New York: Warner Books, 1998), p. 24.

CHAPTER SEVEN

# SPIRITUALITY, CHARACTER AND SELF-CARE

During my (John's) time in Pasadena, Vera Mae and I lived in a neighborhood that had more than its share of crime, most of it related to drugs. One particular drug kingpin, a man known as "Ray Ray," was linked to several killings. He was finally convicted and sent to prison, but this did not prevent him from continuing to run his drug business—and if he put out the word that someone was to be killed, his order was usually carried out.

This was no small concern to us, as the stand our ministry took against drug dealers was common knowledge. Ray Ray, however, had children, some of whom benefited from our ministries. Recognizing that the Harambee Christian Family Center was making a positive difference in the lives of his children, Ray Ray eventually put out the word that no one was to mess with the Perkins family or the Harambee ministry.

THE VALUE OF MODELING AND MENTORING IS THAT OTHERS GET TO SEE HOW WE LIVE—WHICH GIVES THEM THE OPPORTUNITY TO ADOPT OUR POSITIVE, HEALTHY HABITS AND PRACTICES AS THEIR OWN.

Never underestimate the influence your positive example has on others, even convicted killers! It could save your life. More often, the value of modeling and mentoring is that others get to see how we live—which gives them the opportunity to adopt our positive, healthy habits and practices as their own. (Of course, it also gives them the opportunity to observe and imitate our negative habits—but we'll address this later on.) Modeling and mentoring are especially important in the areas of spirituality, character and self-care, which includes caring for our families.

## Maintaining Healthy Spirituality

As ministry leaders, it can be easy to get caught up with starting programs, going to meetings, drafting budgets, planning church services and events, and a long list of other activities, but it's important to remember that our ultimate goal is to bring other people into a relation-

ship with Jesus Christ and to help them grow in that relationship. In our experience, the most effective way to stay true to that goal is to devote ourselves to nurturing our own relationships with Christ, and then to model those relationships for the people around us.

We're not talking here about bragging about how spiritual we are. It's more about engaging in a vibrant spiritual life and then communicating to those we are developing the ways that healthy spirituality makes a significant contribution toward accomplishing our personal and ministry goals. A vibrant spiritual life, among many other things, helps leaders to remain on an even keel and to ward off discouragement when progress seems slow or non-existent.

As with all other areas of growth, relationship with Christ is a lifetime journey. There is always room for us to learn and mature. This relationship is strongest when it is built around daily, intentional time alone with the Lord—when our personal fellowship with Him becomes as much a part of our daily routines as brushing our teeth or eating breakfast, and when we understand that it is as valuable to us as breathing.

There is no one right way to spend time with God. Some people use devotional guides. Some read and reflect on a chapter of a book each day. Others might use this time to read through the Bible or to focus on a particular portion of Scripture. Some do all of the above at one time or another.

Many have made journaling a regular feature of their daily time with God. This entails simply writing down thoughts, joys, frustrations, challenges, insights, and more. It doesn't matter if you don't consider yourself a good writer; chances are no one but you will ever read what you've written anyway. What's important is not the end product, but the process. Journaling helps us, in the immediate presence of God, to become more aware of what is going on around us and to clarify our own thoughts and feelings.

As a brief aside for those of us who preach, some people maintain that we should keep our personal devotional lives separate from our sermon preparation. This is really a matter of personal preference and case-by-case discernment. There may be times when our devotional experience becomes so personal that the insights are not relevant to or appropriate for a larger audience. As a general rule, however, we see no reason the two can't mix. In fact, it seems to make sense to share with

the congregation insights that emerge from daily devotions—if for no other reason than that making reference in a sermon to daily devotional time helps to communicate the importance of time alone with God.

The amount of time spent alone with God can vary. It might be 15 minutes or 3 hours. It may vary from day to day, based on a number of circumstances. Rather than a specific amount of time, what we believe is important is the presence of three S's: solitude, Scripture and silence.

SOLITUDE MEANS MORE THAN THE ABSENCE OF OTHER PEOPLE; IT ALSO INCLUDES THE ABSENCE OF DISTRACTIONS.

Solitude, of course, is prerequisite to time alone with God. If there are other people around, then we're not really alone. But solitude means more than the absence of other people; it also includes the absence of distractions such as television, buzzing cell phones, and fussing children. What's more, it means—for a brief period of time—setting aside the worries of the day. "Be still," Scripture exhorts, "and know that I am God" (Ps. 46:10). As difficult as it may be, we are to put our focus on Him—not on the countless things that clamor for our attention. If it's tempting to dismiss the importance of alone time with God, consider this: "Very early in the morning, while it was still dark, Jesus got up, left the house and went off to a solitary place, where he prayed" (Mark 1:35). As accessible as He was to people most of the time, Jesus made room in His life for alone time with the Father. As we follow His example of servant leadership, it is wise for us to do the same.

For obvious reasons, Scripture should be a regular feature of daily devotional time. Although there is disagreement in some areas of interpretation, the Bible's basic messages are clear—and the more we dwell on those messages, the more they will shape our attitudes and behavior. Meditating on Scripture can also lead to guidance and insights relating to situations and challenges we are facing in our lives and ministries.

For this to happen, however, requires practicing the third S, which is silence—not just an absence of noise, but silence for the purpose of

listening. Especially early in our Christian walks, it can be easy for us to define prayer in terms of pouring out our burdens, confessing our sins, and asking God for things we want or feel we need—and these are all valid and important elements of a prayer life. However, mature spirituality also places an emphasis on listening—seeing prayer as a two-way conversation between us and God. We likely won't hear God's side of the conversation audibly. But we can expect Him to calm our spirits, shape our perspectives, and mold our attitudes.

MATURE SPIRITUALITY PLACES AN EMPHASIS ON LISTENING—ON SEEING PRAYER AS A TWO-WAY CONVERSATION BETWEEN US AND GOD.

## The Importance of Moral Character

During the civil rights movement, I (John) worked with all sorts of people in pursuit of freedom and justice—and I appreciated all of them for their dedication to the cause. But I was most drawn to those who, in addition to pursuing the movement's specific goals, lived morally upright lives. In most cases, this was rooted in their commitment to Christ and to biblical principles. Faith-based moral character became an essential part of my philosophy of wholistic ministry and Christian community development.

I've been developing leaders for about 50 years now, starting at Voice of Calvary Ministries in Mendenhall, Mississippi, in the early 1960s, and I've always stressed how important it is for those who want to be leaders to have strong moral character. Now, I'm a pretty candid kind of guy, so I don't mind addressing issues that some are uncomfortable talking about. For many men, especially those who are on the road a lot, the main issue is sex. I always tell the men I'm training or mentoring that they need to be aware of the temptations they will face so that they can keep the promises they've made and preserve their integrity as leaders.

Moral character and effective leadership are inseparably related. Therefore, setting a moral compass constitutes a crucial aspect of leadership development. Without such grounding, it doesn't matter how much a person has in terms of skills or natural leadership ability. Somewhere along the way, such a leader's moral failings will undermine all that has been accomplished through his or her leadership. We don't think it's too much to say that developing leaders who have no moral compass plants seeds for disaster.

Jesus modeled, among many other things, moral character that was rooted in integrity and honesty. In stark contrast to the moral relativism that is common today, His teachings regularly pointed out the difference between right and wrong—and the importance of choosing right.

This is not to say that leaders can be perfect—or that we should try to present ourselves in that light. We all struggle and make mistakes. We go through hard times. We need the forgiveness and help of others. But there is a huge difference between coming up short from time to time and being guilty of major moral lapses. Our goal is to model lives that, while not perfect, are inclined toward God—toward what is good, holy, righteous and just. We recognize that the capacity to influence is severely compromised by major moral failure. Those whose moral character is fundamentally flawed cannot speak prophetically to the Church or to the community.

Richard Foster, in a single book title, captured the essence of the greatest temptations leaders face: *Money, Sex and Power*. To deny that we face each of these temptations to one degree or another is a mistake. The temptations tend to increase in intensity as we climb the leadership ladder. If we are not careful, our heads can get a little bigger than they ought to. The more we have praise heaped upon us for all we have accomplished, the more likely we are to think we are invulnerable to criticism, that we're entitled to more than we deserve, and that we can't do anything wrong—or at least, that we won't get caught.

One of the Old Testament's most morally flawed characters is King David. Yes, he slew Goliath and wrote some powerful psalms, but he was also an adulterer and a murderer. Clearly, those parts of his story are not included in the Bible as an example for us to follow. Rather, they are included as a stop sign. David's story reminds us that we are

all flawed; we are all susceptible to moral failure. If it could happen to God's anointed king—the one described as "a man after [God's] own heart" (Acts 13:22)—then it can happen to any of us.

Instead of thinking we are immune to temptation, the wiser approach is to acknowledge our vulnerability and then take precautions—safeguards designed to protect our moral character. For example, when we travel with others, we can choose to share a hotel room. A man is not likely to turn on some pornography channel if a friend and brother is staying there in the room with him. Jesus routinely sent the disciples out two by two (see, for example, Mark 6:7). It's likely that one of the reasons was that they could protect each other and hold each other accountable while they were on the road.

INSTEAD OF THINKING WE ARE IMMUNE TO TEMPTATION, THE WISER APPROACH IS TO ACKNOWLEDGE OUR VULNERABILITY AND THEN TAKE PRECAUTIONS.

The best strategy, when seeking to avoid and resist temptation, is not to wait until we encounter certain situations to determine what we will do, but rather to have a solid moral foundation in place in advance so that we can move forward with confidence that there are certain things we simply will not do. In addition, if we know we are especially vulnerable in certain areas, common sense dictates that we should steer clear of those areas. If a person has a drinking problem, he or she is probably better off not going into bars, while those who struggle with gambling may want to steer clear of casinos.

In striving to do what is right, it helps to think of the people in our lives with whom we are closest—those whom we love the most, and whom we least want to hurt. Think about the spouse or child you will have to face when your moral failure comes to light. (Because despite what some believe, it *will* come to light.) Thinking in advance of the pain a bad choice would cause can serve as strong motivation to make a better one.

Over the years, we have learned to communicate openly and honestly with our spouses, and they have always been willing to help us process whatever temptation or struggle we are going through and to offer support and advice. We are convinced that marriages are strongest when husbands and wives keep no secrets from each other—when each knows where the other is and what he or she is doing at all times. Any husband who feels he has to keep a secret from his wife—who finds himself lying about who was on the other end of the phone call, or whom he is going out to meet—already has a problem.

In short, it's vital for leaders to fight temptation with the constant awareness of the long-term consequences of their actions. This includes, as noted, the recognition that effective leadership and moral character are inseparably related.

IT'S VITAL FOR LEADERS TO FIGHT TEMPTATION WITH THE CONSTANT AWARENESS OF THE LONG-TERM CONSEQUENCES OF THEIR ACTIONS.

A final note on this topic: It's important for leaders to take precautions to guard against not only actual impropriety but also the appearance of wrongdoing. Perception can go a long way toward damaging a reputation—so spending time after hours in a closed room with someone of the opposite gender or making a lunch date with someone who is not your spouse can quickly become problematic, even if the interactions themselves were not inappropriate. With this in mind, windows and open doors can go a long way toward guarding a leader's reputation.

## Self-Care

One of the greatest challenges for many people in ministry leadership positions is finding the right balance between taking care of themselves and serving others. It may be helpful to realize that these two aims are not in competition with each other. In fact, the more we succeed at the first, the better we will do at the second.

Anyone who has been on an airplane has heard the flight attendant remind passengers that, in the case of an emergency, they should make sure their own oxygen masks are in place before assisting others. At first, this instruction seems to advocate selfishness. But the logic behind it is that a person won't be able to help others for very long if that person can't breathe. Likewise, leaders have physical and emotional needs and limitations. A pastor who ends up hospitalized because of physical or mental exhaustion isn't helping anyone, no matter how loving and caring he or she might be.

Leaders, not just for our own sake, but also for the sake of those we are serving, need to recognize how important it is to take care of ourselves. It's good for us to read books just for fun, to play games and follow our favorite sports teams, and to go on picnics and camping expeditions. God intends for His people to enjoy life. That's why He gave us rules to live by but freedom within those rules. If we want others to understand that life is meant to be enjoyed, then we can start by showing them that we are capable of relaxing and having fun.

## Rediscovering Sabbath

Did you know that the commandment to keep the Sabbath is the longest of the Ten Commandments? God explained it more than any of the others. Yet it's the one that many Christians, including leaders, seem to ignore. Imagine if a leader of some Christian ministry developed a routine of lying to people or stealing from the ministry. That person would be held accountable. Not so with breaking the Sabbath.

In our lives as leaders, we will benefit from discovering or rediscovering the importance of keeping the Sabbath. The concept of Sabbath was present even before the fall of Adam and Eve. God rested on the seventh day of creation. Resting is part of the rhythm of life. We can survive without keeping the Sabbath—and perhaps even thrive to some extent. But over the long haul, we will be better equipped spiritually, emotionally and physically if we practice Sabbath.

This is a tough adjustment for many leaders to make, because leaders tend to be workaholics. There is always something else to do, or someone else to call. We feel we can't afford to take any time off. It took me (Wayne) 25 years of ministry to fully get it—to completely

understand the importance of keeping the Sabbath and how it could make me a better person and a more effective leader. This is one of those areas where I say to others, "Don't do what I did. Make Sabbath a part of your life right now."

For the last 10 years, Anne and I have made Fridays our Sabbath. It's our time to rest. We spend part of the morning just sitting around, drinking coffee and catching up. We have an extended time of devotions and prayer. The cell phones get turned off. No calling or texting. No checking email. No meetings or working on projects. For three and a half hours every Friday morning, we simply share our lives with each other and with God.

In addition to spending Sabbath time with their spouses, if they have them, leaders may want to consider being part of a group outside the church or ministry. We have found it useful to get together with other men at least monthly, if not once a week. (We imagine that female leaders would find it similarly helpful to gather with other women.) This is a time to share joys and challenges, to support one another in prayer, to learn together, to get advice, and to hold one another accountable. People who care about you but have a bit of a distance from your situation can often provide new insights and perspectives. Getting such a fresh take on things can be wonderfully restful and reinvigorating.

## Family Care

It's a bit hypocritical for us as leaders to tell others to take care of their families if we are not taking care of our own. I (Wayne) will never forget an experience Anne and I had more than 20 years ago, when our three children were very young. We sat them down and asked them what, if anything, they would change about us. They focused on Anne first. They didn't have much to say, except that sometimes she could get a little grouchy when they got home from school.

I was expecting to get off just as easy, if not easier. Instead, I got a revelation. Angela, my daughter, said to me, "Dad, the thing I would change about you is that I don't trust you."

Surprised, I asked her, "What do you mean?" I remember thinking, *I'm a pastor. I always tell you the truth. I'm honest with everyone.*

Angela responded, "You always tell me you are going to do something, and then you never do it."

IT'S A BIT HYPOCRITICAL FOR US AS LEADERS TO TELL OTHERS TO TAKE CARE OF THEIR FAMILIES IF WE ARE NOT TAKING CARE OF OUR OWN.

Those were hard words for me to hear. But there was more. Andrew took his turn: "The thing I would change about you is that you would be around more. You're never around; you're never home."

After that conversation, I began to make some changes. I was both hurt and challenged by what my children said to me, and I wanted to improve. It occurred to me that I didn't really know how to be a good husband or a good father. I started trying to be home more, especially at night. But old habits and patterns were hard to break, and I didn't solve the problem immediately. I would tell Anne I'd be home at a certain time and then get stopped by two or three people who wanted to talk about something. This sent the message to my family that other people were more important to me than they were. Although I made improvements, I didn't address the problem completely until I came to full appreciation, as mentioned above, of the importance of Sabbath.

It's vital for leaders to understand that spending time with our spouses and children is not something we do instead of ministry. Rather, it is something we do as a part of ministry. Not only are we faithfully loving and serving people whom God has entrusted to us, but we also demonstrate this value to those we are developing—encouraging them, without having to say a word, to make the same commitment to their own families.

Although we have treated them somewhat as distinct topics, spirituality, moral character and self-care are closely related to one another. Spending time with God daily builds the strength and wisdom needed to maintain moral character, while healthy and vibrant relationships with family members provide motivation for moral accountability. As we invest in each area, we will see fruit in the others as well—and such

investment is certainly worth the time and effort. Growing spiritual maturity, moral character, and a commitment to self-care all have vital roles to play in the leadership revolution.

CHAPTER EIGHT

# THE CRUCIAL ROLE OF MENTORING

Joseph "Joe Joe" Atkins, Jr. is a former drug addict and one of the founding members of Lawndale Community Church. When I (Wayne) met Joe Joe, he was a high school student. At that time, he volunteered his services as a bodyguard for Anne. We began to pour our lives into this young man, and after a while, Anne invited him to be part of the church's Stephen Ministry. (Stephen Ministries is a national organization that focuses on caring for people within and outside the church congregation.) Joe Joe accepted the invitation, and that was a significant step on the road to bigger and better things—including founding LCC's Hope House Ministry, which focuses on helping men re-enter society after prison or drug addiction. Joe Joe, who has been drug-free, as of this writing, for 17 years, serves as Hope House's director.

Joe Joe is one of a number of people we have chosen to build our lives around in an intentional effort to mentor potential leaders. His story is told more completely in *Real Hope in Chicago*, but even this brief description bears witness to what is possible when leaders take young people under their wings and invest deeply in their lives. To this day, Joe Joe is a regular guest at the Gordon home. I've taken him with me on trips around the country. In the summer of 2012, Anne and I took a trip to Africa, and Joe Joe, along with his 12-year-old daughter, Jamila Wayne (named after one of this book's authors!), went with us. (As you can see, we still "don't go anywhere alone"!)

IT IS AMAZING WHAT IS POSSIBLE WHEN LEADERS TAKE YOUNG PEOPLE UNDER THEIR WINGS AND INVEST DEEPLY IN THEIR LIVES.

In addition to his leadership at Hope House, Joe Joe was a catalyst for another important ministry initiative at Lawndale. He felt called to get formal training in order to become a more effective pastor, but a number of barriers stood in his way. He didn't have the right educational background, the time, or the money to complete a traditional

seminary program. Because of Joe Joe, Lawndale partnered with Northern Seminary to offer an eight-course certificate program in urban ministry, designed for those who do not have a college education. This partnership eventually led to Masters and Doctoral programs in Christian community development, which has given us (both John and Wayne) the opportunity to build our lives into the lives of more than 50 African-American pastors (and counting). It was sheer joy to see Joe Joe walk across the stage in his cap and gown, because none of this would have happened without him.

> SOME LEADERS THINK THAT ONCE THEY HAVE "ARRIVED," THEY NO LONGER NEED A MENTOR. NOTHING COULD BE FURTHER FROM THE TRUTH.

We are far from alone in our belief in the power and potential of mentoring. George Hancock-Stefan, a professor at Palmer Seminary of Eastern University in Philadelphia, was once asked what one piece of advice he would offer to his students, if he could know that what he said would remain with them for a lifetime. His response was: "I would offer words of wisdom spoken by Dr. Howard Hendricks in a chapel service at Wheaton College. He said that each of us should have a Timothy and a Paul. A Timothy is a person into whom you pour your life and one you love as you love your own life. A Paul is a mentor from whom you keep no secrets and who can, on the one hand, tell you how bright and wonderful you are and, on the other, correct you when you do stupid things."

Some leaders think that once they have "arrived," they no longer need a mentor—that once they've secured that ideal job or the leadership position they've dreamed about all their lives, they suddenly know everything and no longer need anyone in their lives to give counsel or offer support. Nothing could be farther from the truth. Remember that the best leaders are people who never stop growing—and the

purpose of mentors is to help us grow. In fact, there's nothing wrong with having more than one mentor. It can be beneficial to have several people we trust to shape our thinking and influence our actions in different areas of our lives.

THE BEST LEADERS ARE PEOPLE WHO NEVER STOP GROWING—AND THE PURPOSE OF MENTORS IS TO HELP US GROW.

For many years, John has served as a mentor to me (Wayne). In fact, to say that John Perkins has mentored Wayne Gordon is a monumental understatement. John has poured his life into mine—and continues to do so—about as much as it is possible for one person to share life and wisdom with another. When I hear John preach a sermon, I typically don't find much new in it—not because it's not a good sermon, but because John has already preached it to me at least three or four times!

H. Spees is another mentee in whom John has invested himself deeply. H. came to Mendenhall in 1972, searching for a cause to which he could commit his life. He planned to spend just one summer in Mississippi—working, learning, and developing as a leader. He went back to his native California long enough to get married, and then he and his wife returned to Mendenhall, where they remained for 11 years and started a health center, among other ministries. The mentee has become the mentor, as to this day H. remains a passionate supporter of Christian community development efforts and a prime mover in the arena of leadership foundations.

Earlier, we focused on Jesus' role as a developer of leaders at many different levels. He sought to teach and develop the masses. He worked with groups of several dozen followers. He chose 12 men to be set apart from all others, and from those it appears He was especially close to 3. It's fair to say that Jesus served as a mentor to the 12, and perhaps especially to the 3. He poured His life into them—letting them follow

everywhere He went, offering special insight into the meaning of His teaching, and sharing with them what they could expect to happen in the future.

Pursuing a leadership revolution built on Jesus' example means looking for opportunities to mentor those whose hearts are open and whose capacity to lead can be enhanced astronomically if only they receive some special attention. If each of us identifies a handful of people—perhaps only two or three—into whom we will pour our lives in a special way, we will see remarkable results. If we are truly committed to following Jesus' model, some of these people will be young men and women whose opportunities in life have previously been limited.

PURSUING A LEADERSHIP REVOLUTION BUILT ON JESUS' EXAMPLE MEANS MENTORING THOSE WHOSE HEARTS ARE OPEN AND WHOSE CAPACITY TO LEAD CAN BE ENHANCED IF THEY RECEIVE SOME SPECIAL ATTENTION.

## The Elements of Mentoring

In many sectors of the business world, mentoring is a common and well-defined concept, featuring two major elements. First, the mentor passes on to the mentee the information and skills—the so-called secrets of leadership—that the mentee will need in order to thrive in that particular line of business. (Some of these secrets and skills may be transferable to other areas in life or work.)

The second main function of the mentor, related to the first, is to sponsor the mentee by finding places in the company for him or her to practice or apply the principles that have been shared. The mentoring process includes hands-on experience under the tutelage of the mentor, who continues to serve in the role of coach or advisor. Eventually, the time comes for the mentee to go it alone. At some point, he or she might become a mentor to someone else. In this way, conventional business wisdom gets passed from generation to generation.

When it comes to mentoring in the context of Christian ministry, there is no need to re-invent the wheel. The model that exists in the business world can serve us well. The challenge comes not with knowing what to do or how to do it. The challenge comes with doing it, which entails an intentional, proactive effort to enter into a mentoring relationship with a defined process and goals or outcomes in mind. Sometimes those goals can be quite specific. For example: "I'm going to teach you everything you need to know about our Christian education program so that one day you will become its leader." Other times, we may mentor someone with regard to general knowledge and leadership skills without knowing exactly where that might lead. Whether we are mentoring in a general sense or for a particular purpose, let's remember that the process includes putting people to work—giving them assignments, just as Jesus gave assignments to those He was developing to lead the Church.

MENTORING INCLUDES PUTTING PEOPLE TO WORK—GIVING THEM ASSIGNMENTS, JUST AS JESUS GAVE ASSIGNMENTS TO THOSE HE WAS DEVELOPING TO LEAD THE CHURCH.

Building on the idea that we all need both a Timothy and a Paul in our lives, it makes sense to encourage those we are mentoring to find someone else—usually someone younger—to mentor. Besides giving them opportunities to exercise the leadership skills they've already learned and grow in confidence as leaders, knowing and experiencing what is involved in the mentoring process from the perspective of the mentor can help people become better mentees—and learn even more.

While mentoring and modeling are related concepts, they are not identical. Modeling is an important part of mentoring, but mentoring goes far beyond modeling in that it is both more intentional and more intense. Still, it's fair to say that those who are most in need of a good mentoring relationship are those who have had few if any helpful role models in their lives. In North Lawndale, and in other urban commu-

nities throughout the country, many children grow up in single-parent homes. Often the single parent, usually the mother, is emotionally unavailable to her children—and sometimes physically as well, especially if she works one or more jobs to support the family.

In these settings, not surprisingly, children typically struggle with low self-esteem (as do many young people growing up in other types of environments). A person's self-concept affects his or her capacity to lead effectively. Thus, positive affirmation plays a crucial role in the mentoring process. As part of the formal leadership development program we ran at Lawndale (we'll discuss this in more detail later), we began each class by looking students in the eye and saying, "You are a leader." It was a simple but very important practice—and we could see that it made a difference. Do not underestimate the importance of repetition and continued reinforcement in helping people view themselves more and more as leaders.

## The Fruits of Success

Choosing to mentor those who seem to have the odds stacked against them offers a variety of rewards. For one thing, when such persons rise to positions of leadership, they usually make excellent mentors to others.

CHOOSING TO MENTOR THOSE WHO SEEM TO HAVE THE ODDS STACKED AGAINST THEM OFFERS A VARIETY OF REWARDS.

They can, in all honesty and candor, say to someone else who is struggling and striving to overcome various hardships, "I was once where you are. I know what it's like to grow up without a dad. I've lived in poverty. I've been homeless. I've had a child out of wedlock. I've been addicted to drugs. I've had more DUIs than I can count. I saw a friend

get killed on the street, and I had no one to talk to about it. If you're going through something, chances are I went through it, too. But guess what? Look where I am now. Look how far I've come! I'm not going back either. So don't you look back. Look at me instead. Look ahead. You have a bright future, including a future as a leader. And I'm going to hold your hand so we can walk into that future together."

Another benefit of mentoring those who come from difficult circumstances is the sheer joy that results from seeing someone's life turned completely around through the power of Christ working in the Church. Many disappointments and frustrations come with the territory when ministering in tough urban areas. But the times of joy and celebration make it all worthwhile, and at Lawndale we have experienced many such times over the years.

MANY DISAPPOINTMENTS AND FRUSTRATIONS COME WITH THE TERRITORY WHEN MINISTERING IN TOUGH URBAN AREAS. BUT THE TIMES OF JOY AND CELEBRATION MAKE IT ALL WORTHWHILE.

We've already introduced you to one of the young men we've developed as a leader and who has been a source of great joy—our dear friend Joe Joe. Another person whom I (Wayne) have built my life around for the last 10 years is Darryl Saffore. Darryl was strung out on drugs for several years. He came through Hope House, after which he graduated to the Nehemiah Discipleship House, where the focus is on long-range planning and goal setting. Today, Darryl serves as the executive pastor at Lawndale Community Church. Each week, I spend an hour of focused time with Darryl. He's earned a Master of Divinity degree and is now enrolled in a doctoral program—a program in Christian community development that John and I direct—at Northern Baptist Theological Seminary. Darryl has developed into a strong leader with an impressive set of skills.

Another of Lawndale's great success stories is Chelsea Johnson. Chelsea came to the church as a little girl. A lot of people wondered if she would ever make it. She grew up in poverty. Her mother, Reba, whose relationship with the Lord was on and off, was addicted to drugs. Her father was not around. She and her mother were homeless for a while.

Chelsea considered the church her home, and the people of the church considered her part of the family. We prayed for Chelsea and supported her through her grammar school and high school years. We helped her get through college, visiting her and sending care packages. In her later years, Reba came back to Christ, and the church helped her purchase her own home.

Just when things seemed to be going great for Chelsea, who now had a job and was living in her own apartment, life took a negative turn. Reba had taken custody of her sister's 4 young children. Then she got cancer and died. The children were slated to become wards of the state—unless Chelsea took them in. So that's what she did, instantly becoming a single mother of 4 children—5 years old and under—at the tender age of 27.

That's when we began to build our lives into Chelsea's life even more extensively. I say "we," but it was mostly Anne. She became Chelsea's mentor. They went on shopping trips together. Anne regularly offered guidance in all areas of life, from cooking to mothering. Our daughter, Angela, also came alongside Chelsea, babysitting the kids so Chelsea could have an occasional night out. We had Chelsea and her children over regularly for dinner. In the months after Reba died, we spent Thanksgiving, Christmas and Easter with Chelsea and her family. At Christmas, we made sure the children had presents to open.

The church's relationship with Chelsea went far beyond helping someone in need. We were developing her, sometimes without even realizing it, as a leader. In spite of all the obstacles she faced, Chelsea had something inside of her—a resilience and determination in her heart—that would not allow her to give up.

As a child, Chelsea learned a poem titled "Hey Black Child" by Useni Eugene Perkins. She recited this poem with great enthusiasm in church literally hundreds of times—no exaggeration. It's not an

overstatement to say that this poem, with its message of hope and affirmation, functioned as a lifeline for Chelsea. She recited it for the whole church, but she may have been the one who most needed to hear and to be comforted and encouraged by it. Each time Chelsea proclaimed, "Hey Black Child, do you know who you are? Who you really are? Do you know you can be what you want to be? If you try to be what you can be . . ." she came to believe in herself just a little bit more.[1]

This poem encouraged and inspired other children as well. Chelsea became a role model for kids (and even for many adults) at the church. People watched her grow through high school and college. She started going to seminars and leading Bible studies. At some point, Chelsea stopped reciting "Hey Black Child" and started reciting the poem "Phenomenal Woman" by Maya Angelou. As Chelsea would near the end of the poem, declaring, "Now you understand just why my head's not bowed. I don't shout or jump about or have to talk real loud. When you see me passing it ought to make you proud," it was as if the poem had been written especially for her.

Indeed, Chelsea Johnson, despite all she has faced in life—or perhaps because of all she has faced—has become a truly phenomenal woman. Chelsea met, dated and eventually married Carl Johnson, a man from our church. It was a spectacular wedding, with more than 400 people in attendance. John, who had contributed to Chelsea's development all along, co-officiated the ceremony with me. It was an exciting and fulfilling moment for the church, as we shared this special occasion with our "little girl"—now a strong, mature woman. With the support of a loving community, Chelsea had faced her challenges, fears and temptations, and had conquered them all.

Today, as the senior pastor's assistant and a member of the health center's board, Chelsea possesses superior organizational skills and has become one of Lawndale Community Church's most influential and significant leaders. She is involved in all of the church's key decisions. She has deep roots in the congregation and in the Lawndale community, and her love for both could not be greater. Chelsea is a shining example of both the importance and potential

of mentoring. She—along with Joe Joe, Darryl and many others—is at the center of the leadership revolution.

**Note**

1. Useni Eugene Perkins, *Hey Black Child and Other Children's Poems* (Chicago: Association for the Positive Development of Black Youth, 2003).

CHAPTER NINE

# EMPOWERING OTHERS TO LEAD

Among Lawndale's many unsung heroes is a man named Thomas Worthy. He and his wife, Tracy, live in Lawndale and have been part of the church's ministry for some 20 years. For the last 15 years, without fanfare and unknown to most of the people in the church, Thomas has led a Bible study every Friday morning at 6:30 A.M. for the men at Hope House—men who are struggling to overcome addictions and to get their lives back on track.

Thomas, who chairs our deacon board, considers this more than a duty. He works very hard to make sure that the Bible studies he leads are both current and relevant for the men he serves.

IF WE WANT PEOPLE TO BECOME LEADERS, IT'S IMPORTANT TO START TREATING THEM LIKE LEADERS.

Several men who once lived in Hope House—Jerry Bolden, Darrin Brown and Wardell Tate, among others—now lead Bible studies on other days of the week. For those of us who are working to develop leaders, this is a shining example of success: Men who through the power of Christ have found victory over drugs and alcohol, and have been empowered to help others overcome. All they needed to succeed as leaders was the opportunity to prove themselves.

Goethe put it this way: "Treat people as if they were what they ought to be and you help them to become what they are capable of being." In other words, if we want people to become leaders, it's important to start treating them like leaders and empowering them with the authority and knowledge they require to expand their leadership abilities.

## Creating an Empowering Culture

Leadership development is, at its core, the process of empowerment. It entails a major commitment of time, energy and, often, financial resources. The first step in empowering leaders is to create a culture

in which all people understand that they are important, that their opinions matter, and that their recommendations, whether or not they are eventually adopted, will always get a hearing (and not just a token hearing).

In an empowering culture, those of us who have titles and are over others on the organizational chart recognize that we are not the only ones who have ideas. In fact, as we often remind people, it's usually the case that those who are closest to the problem being addressed or the goal being pursued have the best idea about how to proceed. A culture that promotes the empowerment of others differs radically from the kind of culture in which the leaders are big shots—and where it's clear, the minute you walk in the door, who those big shots are.

We build an empowering culture when we allow others to participate in the decision-making process. We build an empowering culture when we model servant leadership, and when we promote others' self-esteem. We build this culture when we encourage aspiring leaders to write personal mission statements so they can be clear about their purposes and single-minded in their pursuits.

LEADERSHIP DEVELOPMENT IS, AT ITS CORE, THE PROCESS OF EMPOWERMENT. IT ENTAILS A COMMITMENT OF TIME, ENERGY, AND, OFTEN, FINANCIAL RESOURCES.

When working to build an empowering culture—one in which all people feel affirmed as growing leaders—we recommend being as creative and ambitious as possible. Following are just a few examples of things we have done and continue to do at Lawndale to promote a culture that empowers people to lead—and to lead more effectively.

When we worship on Sunday mornings, we don't have any special seats. We don't have a platform, an altar or a stage. Everybody in the congregation sits together as a group. Guided by 1 Corinthians 12, we consider ourselves one body with many parts, none of which is more

important than any other part. When it's time for someone to exercise his or her gift, that person goes up front to read Scripture or sing or preach—and then returns to his or her seat. Those who are in the choir come out of the congregation to sing, and then they go back to the congregation for the remainder of the service.

We also foster a culture of teamwork and unity through our nomenclature. So, for example, in general we don't have "committees." Instead we have "teams," such as the Worship Team or Praise Team.

When for one reason or another a spotlight shines on Lawndale in a positive way, we make an effort to spread that light around so that it's not just a few people getting all the recognition and whatever glory comes with it. For example, not long after former White House Chief of Staff Rahm Emanuel became mayor of Chicago in May 2011, he visited Lawndale to gain an understanding of our church and its ministries, and to discuss how we could work together in pursuit of common goals. As you can imagine, this was quite an exciting opportunity for us! We decided that instead of just having a few people sit and talk with the mayor, we would go around to all of our different ministries. Not only would this give the mayor a clearer picture of our work, but it would also give a number of leaders within the organization a chance to represent the ministry and be affirmed for their hard work and accomplishments.

Our first stop was Hope House. Joe Joe shared with the mayor what was happening there and introduced him to some of the men participating in the program. Then we went on to our learning center, the art center, the youth center, the development corporation, the fitness center, and the legal and health centers. In each location, the people responsible for carrying out these ministries described their work and answered the mayor's questions. As we moved from place to place, we introduced the mayor to everyone we met along the way. For instance, in the learning center, the mayor met with director Pam McCain, who in turn introduced him to one of our volunteers, a young man named Terrell. Before long, the mayor was asking Terrell about his goals in life and offering advice about where Terrell should go to college and what degree he might want to pursue. (The following summer, Terrell became one of the most popular teachers in our summer education program for children.)

The opportunity to speak face to face with the mayor of a major city empowers people. It helps them to believe in themselves and to understand how important they are not only to the success of their ministry but also to the very future of our city.

We have sought to apply this same principle within the Christian Community Development Association. Over a five-year period, we (John and Wayne) visited more than 100 cities, teaching the principles of Christian community development. The program for these visits would typically start on a Friday, but we always arranged to arrive early. On Thursdays during this period, we visited at least 500 CCDA member ministries. We learned, among other things, that the people who labor away at these ministries—often with little visible reward—feel affirmed, significant and empowered when they are visited by the leaders of an organization to which they belong.

Back in Lawndale, another way we empower and equip people is by providing opportunities for them to work at jobs in supportive environments. Hope House men, for example, gain valuable work experience at Lou Malnati's Pizzeria. The Malnati family opened their Lawndale location in 1996 as a partnership with LCC and a way to support the community—and although the operation has never been profitable, they have remained faithful in their commitment to provide both a pleasant place for local residents to dine and a way for those coming out of prison or addiction to develop job skills. Among the things workers at Malnati's learn is the importance of showing up for work on time—it seems basic, but unless they make punctuality a habit, employees will have a hard time finding and keeping jobs in the "real world." Once workers demonstrate that they are responsible, they can move up through the ranks. They might start by cleaning dishes or sweeping floors; over time, if it's what they want, they may become shift managers or managers. Others take the job skills and work ethic they have developed at Malnati's and obtain positions elsewhere.

Over the years, we have established other local businesses—among them a welding business, a car wash, and multiple lawn care businesses—and Joe Joe works to link Hope House residents up with jobs at these establishments. In addition, after recently graduating from college, my (Wayne's) son, Austin, started a business selling fresh fruit from a cart here in Lawndale—a valuable service in a "food desert." (As

in many urban communities, fresh fruit and other healthy grocery items aren't easy to come by in our neighborhood.) Hope Fruit now employs two Hope House men. Among the benefits that come with being employed is that people learn how to do such things as starting a bank account and doing their taxes—activities many of us take for granted. Although it may be hard for people coming from a background of privilege to understand it, these are significant steps for those who are trying to turn their lives around.

## Freedom to Fail

In his poem "Cantares," the Spanish poet Antonio Machado wrote, "Caminante, no hay camino, se hace camino al andar." This is typically translated, "Wayfarer, there is no way. The way is made by walking."

Ultimately, leadership is not something that can be mastered in a classroom. Nothing significant or lasting will be accomplished if leadership exists only in theory. Leaders "make our way" by walking, by running, by trying, by doing, by dreaming, by laughing and crying, by risking, and, sometimes, by failing. Many of us, when we look back over our leadership experience, recognize that we learned and grew more as a result of our mistakes than because of our triumphs. With that in mind, it's important that we give the people we are developing as leaders the opportunity and the freedom to fail—for without such opportunities, they will never genuinely have the opportunity to succeed.

NOTHING SIGNIFICANT OR LASTING WILL BE ACCOMPLISHED IF LEADERSHIP EXISTS ONLY IN THEORY.

As we give developing leaders the chance to try new things, it's likely that they will not do as good a job as we have done or could do, mostly because we've been at it longer. But that doesn't mean we were wrong to give them the opportunity. It takes time and practice to be-

come proficient at anything. For the most skilled, accomplished and trusted surgeon, there was a first operation. For the revered college professor, there was a first class; and for the expert trial lawyer, a first case.

AS WE GIVE DEVELOPING LEADERS THE CHANCE TO TRY NEW THINGS, IT'S LIKELY THEY WILL NOT DO AS GOOD A JOB AS WE HAVE DONE. THAT DOESN'T MEAN WE WERE WRONG TO GIVE THEM THE OPPORTUNITY.

For several years now, I (Wayne) have not preached during most of the summer. We don't bring in outside speakers to fill the void. Instead, we give eight people in the congregation who have a desire to preach the opportunity to use their gifts. I critique them lovingly, just as I hope and expect they will do for me when I preach. From the pulpit to all of Lawndale's other areas of ministry, we practice this principle of giving people opportunities to exercise their talents in new and challenging ways.

## Developing a Succession Plan

A difficult but essential question for leaders to ask ourselves is this: What do we care most about? Is it our own career, image or reputation? Or is it the long-term success of the ministry—and, ultimately, the pursuit of Kingdom values? Those who care mainly about themselves will not be overly concerned with what happens when they leave. What they leave behind becomes someone else's problem. In contrast, leaders who are committed to Kingdom values will do whatever they can to make sure that the ministry is capable of carrying on successfully without them.

The commitment to transferring power from one's own administration or generation to the next means being willing and humble enough to let go of power and influence in order to create space for others to accept the reins of leadership and the authority that goes

with it. Servant leaders who have successfully created a culture of empowerment are sharing authority—giving away power—all the time. Even so, they remain in charge of the overall leadership of the organization. Developing a succession plan—and at some point bringing that plan to fruition—goes beyond sharing power. It entails a complete and permanent transfer of leadership.

Working oneself out of a job can be one of the hardest things in life to do. Even when leaders know they should let go—and want to let go—it's not easy to do. Some—many in fact—are not ready when the time comes. They may have avoided preparing others adequately because, deep down, they didn't want someone else to succeed in their absence. That's why it's so important that we search our souls and pray for purity of heart, seeking not our own desires, but rather what the Kingdom requires.

DEVELOPING A SUCCESSION PLAN—AND AT SOME POINT BRINGING THAT PLAN TO FRUITION—GOES BEYOND SHARING POWER. IT ENTAILS A COMPLETE AND PERMANENT TRANSFER OF LEADERSHIP.

Some leaders don't concern themselves with a succession plan because they intend to stay in place for a good long time. The problem with this approach is that nothing in this life is certain. Any leader—regardless of age or physical condition—can be gone tomorrow. There's not a person alive who doesn't know of people whom God called home unexpectedly through a heart attack, a car accident, or some other unexpected tragedy. No one—regardless of age, health, or adherence to safety precautions—is guaranteed even one more breath of life on this earth.

## The Model of Paul and Timothy

Empowering others to lead is a priority in its own right. But as it relates to creating a succession plan, empowering others becomes crucial.

In his correspondence with Timothy, Paul demonstrated many of the principles associated with a good succession plan. Scholars generally believe that Paul wrote 2 Timothy from a Roman prison not long before his death. Through this letter, Paul did everything he could to make sure that the ideals for which he stood and the goals he had pursued would carry on with Timothy, exhorting his protégé, "What you heard from me, keep as the pattern of sound teaching, with faith and love in Christ Jesus" (2 Tim. 1:13). He instructed Timothy to guard the gifts he had been given with the help of the Holy Spirit (see v. 14). He warned Timothy about those things that could throw him off track, urging him to "flee the evil desires of youth" (2:22). Paul continued, "Don't have anything to do with foolish and stupid arguments, because you know they produce quarrels" (2:23). In other words, focus on the important things.

Paul warned Timothy to have nothing to do with certain people, including "lovers of themselves, lovers of money, [and those who were] boastful, proud, [and] abusive" (3:2). He encouraged Timothy to "continue in what you have learned and have become convinced of, because you know those from whom you learned it" (3:14).

We can be virtually certain that this was not the first time Timothy heard these things from his mentor. Paul had been preparing him and empowering him all along. This letter was a final effort, as the time for succession drew near, to reinforce what he had already taught.

EMPOWERING OTHERS TO LEAD IS A PRIORITY IN ITS OWN RIGHT. BUT AS IT RELATES TO CREATING A SUCCESSION PLAN, EMPOWERING OTHERS BECOMES CRUCIAL.

Especially in recent years, at Lawndale Community Church, within the Christian Community Development Association, and at the John and Vera Mae Perkins Foundation, we have made intentional and focused efforts to ensure that others will be able to carry on in our absence without the ministries losing any ground. Within CCDA, we are

passing on leadership in a number of ways. One of those ways is that each year we select a cohort of 25 leaders, ages 25 to 40, from around the country. Over a period of a year and a half, we spend time with these younger leaders at retreats and in other settings, sharing with them key ideas and principles of leadership and leadership development. We make sure to carve out time to spend with them at each annual CCDA conference. We (John and Wayne) are not the only ones who are involved in this effort. Vera Mae and Anne participate as well; so do Noel Castellanos, the CEO of CCDA, and his wife, Marianne.

Chrissy Brooks, from Costa Mesa, Calfornia's Micah Ministry, was in this program's first cohort, and John Phillip Perkins (John's grandson) was in the second. Among the ways Chrissy and John are practicing what they've learned is by co-leading the third cohort.

This program has been in place for four years, so as of this writing about 100 young people have taken part in it. The first year, we had only 30 or so applicants for 25 slots, but more than 100 people applied for the fourth cohort, making the work of the selection committee, which includes representatives from previous cohorts, much more difficult. This is a good problem to have! With each passing year, our confidence in a bright future for CCDA grows.

## Remembering the Nuts and Bolts

It's one thing to give people permission and authority to lead; it's quite another to make sure they have at their disposal all the information and tools they will need to lead successfully when it's their time to take over. To be sure, attitude and self-confidence are extremely important. But attitude and confidence can quickly crumble in the heat of "nuts and bolts" type questions whose answers are hard to find. By "nuts and bolts," we are referring to such practical aspects of leadership as how to structure the organization's finances, how and when to pay the bills, where to find the keys to the buildings, what are the relevant health department regulations for opening a kitchen to outside groups, and much more.

At Lawndale, I (Wayne) found out the hard way that empowering people to lead is not enough. People also need to be equipped.

In 1995, I took a one-year sabbatical leave from the church, primarily for the purpose of helping the Christian Community Development Association reach the next level of visibility and influence. Up to that point, I had done a pretty good job of giving away power so that others could lead in my absence—but in the area of giving people the tools they needed, it turned out I had failed miserably.

IT'S ONE THING TO GIVE PEOPLE PERMISSION AND AUTHORITY TO LEAD; IT'S QUITE ANOTHER TO MAKE SURE THEY HAVE THE INFORMATION AND TOOLS THEY WILL NEED TO LEAD SUCCESSFULLY WHEN IT'S THEIR TIME TO TAKE OVER.

I suppose I could feel good about having created a culture in which people felt free to speak their minds. Some certainly embraced and exercised that freedom. One of those was Andrew Moore, who had been on the football team I coached at Farragut High School and was an original member of Lawndale Community Church. "Coach," Andrew said, "when you went on sabbatical, we were unprepared to lead. It's like you sent us into a football game without any equipment and with no plays."

Things began to crumble, and eventually, two-thirds of the way through my sabbatical year, they fell apart. Dissident voices calling for changes emerged. There was a major money crunch. The board began laying off staff until only one remained: the lead pastor, who was hesitant to make any major changes (a stance for which he took a lot of heat) because I would be gone for only a year.

I came back for a meeting with the board, and it didn't take too long to put things back together and reinstate those who had been dismissed. It also didn't take long for me to realize that, to stay with the football metaphor, I'd fumbled the ball. For the most part, the kinds of problems and issues that had surfaced in my absence could have been prevented. I had given people the authority to lead, but I

hadn't provided them with the tools and the knowledge they needed to fill their new roles.

This was a valuable learning experience for me. First, it reinforced the importance of leaders owning their mistakes—admitting their failures and imperfections. When those we are developing see that we are far from perfect, they are freed from the pressure of always having to get things right.

Second, the experience brought back to my mind something Tom Skinner had shared with me several years earlier. He had said that when he was seeking advice while forming Tom Skinner Associates, people told him that all he had to do was surround himself with people who were faithful. If he did that, he would have nothing to worry about. Tom had told me that this advice was simply not true. I now had the experience to back up his claim, because the problems that surfaced at Lawndale had absolutely nothing to do with a lack of faithfulness on the part of the key players. Of course, faithfulness is a necessary component of ministry success, but faithfulness alone is far from being a sufficient basis for leadership.

WHEN THOSE WE ARE DEVELOPING SEE THAT WE ARE FAR FROM PERFECT, THEY ARE FREED FROM THE PRESSURE OF ALWAYS HAVING TO GET THINGS RIGHT.

Upon returning from my sabbatical, I made a conscious effort to think about all the things I knew and did that others did not know or do. I made it my goal to eliminate the void that would be created if I were totally out of the picture. I began to make sure that other people—many other people—knew the ins and outs of Lawndale and its ministries at least as well as I did.

This is what servant leaders do when they understand that the ministry they are engaged in is about furthering God's kingdom and not about their own success or reputation. They make an effort to think

about what will happen when they leave the scene if their knowledge and skills are not passed on. They do their best to make sure that their ministries will carry on—because they have given other people not only the authority but also the tools and information they need to lead. Today, I'm confident that I could be hit by a car or die of a heart attack tomorrow, and the people in place at Lawndale would be able to pick up the baton and run with it.

SERVANT LEADERS DO THEIR BEST TO MAKE SURE THAT THEIR MINISTRIES WILL CARRY ON—BECAUSE THEY HAVE GIVEN OTHER PEOPLE NOT ONLY THE AUTHORITY BUT ALSO THE TOOLS AND INFORMATION THEY NEED TO LEAD.

## Post-Resurrection Peter

The apostle Peter provides an inspiring example of how someone can grow and develop over time as he is empowered and equipped to lead. In the Gospels, Peter comes across as an energetic and committed disciple, but also as someone who is at times impulsive and at other times weak in his faith. However, in the book of Acts, a portrait of Peter emerges that makes it clear he has learned the essentials and is ready to lead the effort to build the Church of Jesus Christ.

In the first chapter of Acts, it's Peter who stands up among the believers to lead the process of selecting Matthias to replace Judas as an apostle (see vv. 15-26). From that point on, Peter becomes a kind of Jesus figure. That is, he says and does many of the same things Jesus said and did, as recorded by the Gospel writers.

Acts 2 describes Peter addressing the crowd to explain the phenomena associated with Pentecost. He testifies to the resurrected Christ and invites people to "repent and be baptized" (v. 38). Later, Peter heals a crippled beggar and then addresses those who witnessed the miracle, again speaking boldly about Christ (see 3:6-26). This

lands him and John in jail for upsetting the temple guard and Sadducees (see 4:1-3). Peter and John then have to appear before the rulers, elders and teachers of the law, including Annas and Caiaphas—just as Jesus did.

Peter must answer the question, "By what power or what name did you do this?" (Acts 4:7). He responds, "It is by the name of Jesus Christ of Nazareth, whom you crucified but whom God raised from the dead, that this man stands before you healed" (v. 10). Clearly, Peter's days of denying Christ are well behind him.

Just as people wanted to get close to Jesus so they could be healed, we find people "[bringing] the sick into the streets and [laying] them on beds and mats so that at least Peter's shadow might fall on some of them as he passed by" (Acts 5:15). Again, Peter is portrayed in Acts in much the same way Christ is portrayed in the Gospels. In other words, the succession plan has been successfully implemented, and a new generation of leadership is carrying on the ministry entrusted to them.

PETER WAS BY ALL ACCOUNTS A NORMAL GUY—JUST A FISHERMAN WHO HAPPENED TO BE IN THE RIGHT PLACE AT THE RIGHT TIME TO BE CALLED INTO LEADERSHIP.

Let's take just a moment to reflect on what is recorded in Acts 4:13: "When [the authorities] saw the courage of Peter and John and realized that they were unschooled, ordinary men, they were astonished and they took note that these men had been with Jesus."

It's clear that Peter (and John) had no special talent or unique intelligence. Peter was by all accounts a normal guy—just a fisherman who happened to be in the right place at the right time to be called into leadership. But he hung out with Christ. He watched and listened. He paid attention. Yes, Peter made some mistakes, but he learned from those mistakes and moved on. When his time came to

lead, he was fully prepared for the task at hand. This model of empowering others to lead will play an important role in guiding the leadership revolution.

CHAPTER TEN

# FOCUSING ON CHILDREN AND YOUTH

One of the things I (John) like about Wayne is that he's quick to give credit where it's due—including when it's due to young people. It takes humility for a leader to do that. Some might be tempted to claim the good ideas younger folks have as their own. Not Wayne. He'll be the first to tell you how much Lawndale Community Church and its ministry owe to the teenagers who were founding members of the congregation. Here's how he describes one of their great contributions:

> Just a few weeks after we started the church, some high school kids approached me and said, "Coach, you know what? We said we're going to love God and love people, but we aren't doing anything for anybody in our neighborhood. Don't you think, as a church, we ought to love our neighborhood?" It took me only a fraction of a second to realize that yes, of course, God calls churches to love their neighborhoods. We recognized that God was calling us, a little church of fifteen people, to start loving our neighborhood, even though we didn't know for sure where that commitment would lead.[1]

Where it led was to the ministries that today meet people's health care, housing, educational, job-related, addiction recovery, legal and other needs.

IT TAKES HUMILITY FOR A LEADER TO GIVE CREDIT WHERE IT'S DUE—INCLUDING WHEN IT'S DUE TO YOUNG PEOPLE.

In 2012, 19 young people from LCC graduated from high school and went on to college. This is more than the entire population of the church when it first started. But some things haven't changed. I (Wayne) still ask young people for advice. Anne and I lead the eleventh- and twelfth-grade Sunday School class at the church, and when I was invited to speak at a Q conference, I asked our students what they

thought I should talk about. They advised me to address the importance of churches loving their communities and doing community development. I took their advice. Young people keep the rest of us young and current while we strive to ground them in God's Word.

Given what young people contributed to LCC's origins and our ongoing ministry, it's not surprising that we at Lawndale are convinced that any serious commitment to leadership and community development over the long haul must include a commitment to children and youth. Just think what we might have missed out on if we hadn't taken our young people seriously all those years ago!

Of course, all people can become better leaders, and efforts to develop leaders should not exclude those who are older. But an essential component of leadership development is the recognition that some of the toddlers in your church nursery will one day be leaders in the church and the community. One or more of them might end up being the senior pastor. These future leaders will need to be nurtured every step of the way.

Most Christian community development ministries put a strong emphasis on developing youth—winning young people to Christ as early as kindergarten and then following them all the way through college with spiritual and educational nurturing. This is one of the reasons that we recommend to anyone who is considering starting a community development ministry that they commit to staying in that community for at least 15 years.

The most effective community development efforts include ministries to children and youth that are so lively, so dynamic, so meaningful and so fun that they come to occupy the center of these young people's lives. The goal is for church to become something that young people build their lives around, not just something they do on the side. We want them to attend church and church activities not because they have to—some will not even have parents who tell them they have to—but because they want to, and because the church has become so central to their values and to their life goals that they can't imagine not being part of a community of believers.

One of the most common challenges churches—especially so-called mainline churches—face is the tension between old and new ways of doing church. Some members call for change, while others

want things to stay the way they've been for 50 years or more. There are discussions and debates over what music should be a part of the service, and over whether to project words and images onto screens or to use the hymnals. What will it be—the organ or a praise band featuring guitars and snare drums? Whatever the arguments for or against any particular change, we would venture to say that those who look around on Sunday mornings and see mostly heads that are either bald or gray have a problem.

ONE OF THE MOST COMMON CHALLENGES CHURCHES FACE IS THE TENSION BETWEEN OLD AND NEW WAYS OF DOING CHURCH.

Someone once conducted a quick, three-question survey of elderly folk at a particular church. The first question was, "How many of you want to change the Sunday morning service around so that it will be more appealing to young people?" Almost no one raised a hand. The second question was, "How many of you want to have your grandsons and granddaughters sitting next to you at church on Sunday mornings?" Now all the hands went up. The third question was actually a repeat of the first: "How many are open to changing the service?" This time, after having had the chance to consider the second question, everyone raised a hand.

Now, all of this is not to say that the opinions and perspectives of older folks should be disregarded. We happen to be 59 (Wayne) and 82 (John), and although we might be called "chronologically challenged," we like to think we still have a few good ideas in us. Among the lessons we can convey to young people is that they would do well to learn to compromise and that there is much wisdom to be gleaned from those who have been around a bit longer. But intergenerational respect and communication is a two-way street—if we want the young people to consider what we have to say, we'll need to take them seriously as well.

Of course, there will be times when leaders of churches and ministries face situations where compromise is not an option, and they will have to make unpopular decisions. This could involve ways to involve young people in the life of the church, or it could be a decision about how to redecorate its sanctuary. In the wake of these kinds of choices, some members—including perhaps major donors—might leave. This is never what we want to happen, but we find encouragement in remembering that the ultimate goal is not to enable a church to succeed, but to build the kingdom of God.

## Wanted: The Visions of Youth

According to the Gospels, Jesus had more than one opportunity to send the message that children weren't really a part of what He was about. On each of those occasions, He communicated instead that not only were young people invited to the party, but their attitudes and values were also at the very heart of the kingdom of God He was proclaiming.

The truth is that the Church needs young people. When we get tired, we need their energy. When we tend toward cynicism, we need their idealism. When we run out of ideas, we need their fresh perspectives. We need their youthful vision—not to mention their technological expertise when we have a computer problem!

In his book *Just Courage*, Gary Haugen, president and CEO of International Justice Mission (IJM), offers a revealing perspective on the idealism of youth. IJM works mostly in poor countries to free women and children from forced prostitution and slavery. The organization invites Christian youth who are committed to the ministry's goals to participate in various kinds of internships. This sometimes entails going into difficult places overseas—a fact that motivates the young people but scares many of their parents. Haugen writes:

> After we have poured into our children all the good food and shelter and clothing, after we have provided them with great education, discipline, structure and love, after we have worked so hard to provide every good thing, they turn to us and ask, "Why have you given all this to me?"

> And the honest answer from me is, "So you'll be safe."
>
> And my kid looks up at me and says, "Really? That's it? You want me to be safe? Your grand ambition for me is that nothing bad happens?"
>
> And I think something inside them dies. They either go away to perish in safety, or they go away looking for adventure in the wrong places. Jesus, on the other hand, affirms their sense of adventure and their yearning for larger glory. In fact, he is encouraging us to affirm this calling in our children and to raise them up to be brave, to be loving and to be significant. But honestly, sometimes I just want my kids to be safe. And I think they smell my fear, and it builds little prisons that can last a lifetime.
>
> According to Jesus, it doesn't have to be that way. He gives me a role in helping my kids choose to be brave, to be loving and to be significant. In the end, this is the stuff that will change the world.[2]

Because young people represent the Church of tomorrow, those of us who are leaders today have a responsibility to do everything we can to make sure our youth are engaged, connected, and encouraged to follow Christ in bold ways that may, in fact, change the world. We can do this by ensuring that our young people have access to the best and brightest models and mentors. We can do it by building programs and activities around our children and youth in the hope that they will grow and learn, that they will eventually move into positions of leadership, and that, once they do, they will choose to remain in and serve the community that reared them.

## Keeping Young People Engaged

The old saying that children are meant to be seen and not heard has no place in a church that cares about developing future leaders. It doesn't help anyone when children come to church, fold their hands, sit still the whole time, and are bored. It's far better for church to be fun for young people; in fact, to some extent, church services ought to be designed with them in mind. High-quality children's sermons—whose

messages take into consideration children's level of development and the things they find relevant and interesting—will reach young people more effectively than will messages that are geared toward adults with the children merely listening in. If church is not meaningful and fun for children, they will likely abandon it when they're old enough to do so.

IF CHURCH IS NOT MEANINGFUL AND FUN FOR CHILDREN, THEY WILL ABANDON IT WHEN THEY'RE OLD ENOUGH TO DO SO.

At Lawndale, children attend the first half of the adult service. This sends the message that church is for people of all ages, and that it's good for people from different generations to worship together. We don't expect the kids to sit still. They get up and move around; sometimes they dance while the choir is singing. After the children's message, the kids get a healthy snack—an apple—and then go off to junior church, which is designed to be both age appropriate and lots of fun. They leave smiling; going to junior church is a festive occasion. Among other activities, they'll get to hear Christian hip-hop music and view multimedia presentations that build on their likes and interests.

Those who lead programs for children and youth ought to be among the church's most dedicated, creative and energetic people. Someone recently asked for advice on how to handle a situation at a particular church where the junior high youth Sunday School teacher was not connecting with her students. This teacher had been in charge of the class for more than 20 years, and over that time very little had changed with regard to either the content or teaching style. Several youth simply quit going. Those who kept going didn't enjoy the class at all. They were completely bored.

Lots of churches face similar challenges. In this case, the pastor was hesitant to talk with the woman or to make any changes because he didn't want to hurt her feelings. After all, she'd been such a loyal teacher for so long. With all due respect to the pastor's motives and

concerns, at some point it becomes necessary to ask what is more important: a teacher's feelings or the spiritual vitality and growth of the youth. Leadership often entails having to make hard choices. Presumably, this woman's salvation is secure. That might not be the case for the young people the church has the potential to reach. Assuming there are other options—other teachers who will be better able to connect with youth—those options should be exercised.

Of course, the situation needs to be handled with sensitivity. Thank the woman for her years of service; perhaps even hold an event to honor her. Make sure she feels appreciated. Perhaps couch the change as a new direction in youth ministry. Maybe even give the junior high group a new name. Hopefully, as someone who has invested a great deal in young people, this long-time teacher will be able to rejoice in something new and exciting for the youth. But even if she can't, a change has to be made.

Another thing for churches to take a close look at is how space is allocated in their physical facilities. Upon doing so, many will discover that the newer, nicer, more spacious rooms are places where the adults gather, while the older, more rundown, out-of-the-way places are designated for the youth. Churches that spend more money on adults than they do on youth may want to reexamine their priorities. When young people are treated as second-class citizens, they get the message that they're not important. But the fact is, they are vitally important to the success of the leadership revolution.

## Simple Strategies

Knowing how to show love for kids is not rocket science. Investing in their growth often doesn't cost any money, and sometimes doesn't even require much time. At Lawndale, we do a number of simple things—things any church can do—to make sure that our young people feel significant and affirmed as often as possible. One very basic way for adults to help young people feel affirmed and significant is to learn their names. Adults often see the same youth in church week after week. They might greet them, but not by name. All of us feel special when someone calls us by name. Addressing young people by their names can and should be common practice in all churches.

Another way to make our young people feel loved and significant is by touching them as often as possible. In recent years, there has been so much in the news regarding inappropriate physical contact between adults and children or youth that many have forgotten the important role of appropriate touch. How "appropriate touch" is understood can vary to some degree based on culture. But every child ought to be receiving at least a few hugs or pats on the back on Sunday morning.

EVERY CHILD OUGHT TO BE RECEIVING AT LEAST A FEW HUGS OR PATS ON THE BACK ON SUNDAY MORNING.

If you're not much of a hugger, consider that there are other forms of touch as well. A gentle punch in the shoulder or a high-five fist bump can be a great way to connect with a junior high or senior high youth. If a young man you know is walking by you on his way to his seat in church, reach out and give him a little push to take him off his stride. Guaranteed, he'll turn to see who pushed him. Then he'll smile—because he'll take the gesture as a sign that you care.

As we seek to keep youth engaged in the life and ministries of the church, it's helpful to go as often as possible to their events: band concerts and plays, sporting events, choral concerts and science fairs. When we show up at young peoples' activities, it says to them, "I'm here because of you." It shows that the things that matter to them matter to us. A senior pastor can't do it all, but he or she can create a culture in which people recognize the importance of supporting our youth by attending their events.

Though it may take us out of our own comfort zones, it's a good idea for pastors and others to make an effort to connect with young people in the ways young people are comfortable connecting with one another. Be careful not to try to be so hip that you are fake. But there's nothing wrong with sending an occasional text message to remind

someone about the upcoming youth retreat. Or you can ask young people to be your friend on Facebook, making sure they know that you won't be offended if they decline the invitation.

## A Formal Program

These informal, spontaneous methods for connecting with young people and developing future leaders are not meant to replace formal leadership development programs. Every year since the mid-1980s at Lawndale, we have run a summer program called "The Garden." In this program, 125 grammar school kids spend 6 weeks in a classroom setting learning the kinds of skills and adopting the kinds of attitudes that will help them succeed someday as leaders. High school and college students teach the classes. In recent years, the college students have come to us from InterVarsity Christian Fellowship.

> EVERY YOUNG PERSON IN OUR MIDST IS NOT ONLY A REPRESENTATIVE OF THE KINGDOM OF GOD, BUT ALSO A POTENTIAL FUTURE LEADER IN THE CHURCH AND THE COMMUNITY.

This program is a win-win for everyone. For the high school and college students, it's an opportunity for a summer job that enables them to practice their own leadership skills, in part by designing the program each summer. At the same time, the program helps the younger children build confidence; grow in self-esteem; and develop life skills, Christian values and intellectual abilities that will help them when they go back to school in the fall. Some who have come through The Garden program hold positions of leadership at Lawndale today.

What is appropriate and achievable in terms of a formal program will vary from setting to setting. Regardless, we strongly encourage churches and community development ministries to take advantage of both formal and informal opportunities to reach children and youth. Every young per-

son in our midst is not only a representative of the kingdom of God, but also a potential future leader in the church and the community. We can't afford *not* to invest in their growth and development.

**Notes**

1. Wayne Gordon, *Who Is My Neighbor?* (Ventura, CA: Gospel Light, 2010), pp. 22-23.
2. Gary A. Haugen, *Just Courage* (Downers Grove, IL: InterVarsity Press, 2008), pp. 124-125.

CHAPTER ELEVEN

# LEADERSHIP THAT ENGAGES THE WORLD

In the late 1990s, the Chicago Transportation Authority (CTA) made a decision to stop running the El train after midnight, and to eliminate all weekend service. Had these service cuts taken place, they would have created a hardship for many in our city, especially those who worked on weekends or whose shifts ended after midnight. Lawndale Community Church organized a community meeting, which some 2,000 people attended. This led to a petition that had enough signatures to persuade the CTA to reverse its decision.

THE CHURCH IS CALLED TO FEED THE HUNGRY, CLOTHE THE NAKED, VISIT PRISONERS, CARE FOR WIDOWS, AND WORK FOR JUSTICE AND PEACE IN THE WORLD.

Throughout much of this book, we have been focusing on developing leaders for the Church and for Christian ministries, because we believe that the Church represents the best hope for positive change in our society. What greater motivation can there be for working for change than to serve and obey the Creator and Lord of the universe? However, the Church's role is not limited to bringing others to a personal relationship with Jesus Christ, important as that is. We are also called to feed the hungry, clothe the naked, visit prisoners, care for widows, and work for justice and peace in the world.

Justice is primarily a stewardship issue, involving discussion of topics such as how we manage things on earth. Do we do so in ways that enhance or that inhibit life? Injustice includes denying people access to the good things God created. It includes exploiting people—depriving them of the opportunity to reach their full potential in life.

In today's secular society, many have a negative perception of the Church, based partly on the media's aggressiveness in covering scandals involving religious leaders. People often fail to appreciate the extent to which people of faith are carrying out efforts to alleviate pain and suffering in our world.

In developing leaders, the ultimate goal is not to build the Church, but to make disciples and shape our world in the name of Jesus Christ. Yes, we need pastors and deacons and choir directors, but we also need schoolteachers and businesspeople and athletes and carpenters and nurses and many others to stand for Christian values in their places of employment and in the public square. Lawndale Community Church's membership includes doctors, attorneys, policemen, teachers, elected officials, business leaders, and more. Some are already in prominent positions of influence as leaders in the broader community.

There are leaders of society who attend churches all across the country. The goal of the Church is to infuse these leaders with biblical values and to provide inspiration and support so that they are equipped to represent Christian values in their places of influence.

## Boldly Venturing into the Public Square

From the beginning of the Church, believers have made public proclamations of faith. They did not hide their beliefs under a bushel. Acts 4 describes Peter and John being put in jail for "teaching the people and proclaiming in Jesus the resurrection of the dead" (vv. 2-3). Upon their release, they were warned "not to speak or teach at all in the name of Jesus" (v. 18). But they did it anyway. Christianity is not a reclusive religion.

PART OF OUR CALLING AS FOLLOWERS OF JESUS IS TO ENGAGE THE WORLD AT EVERY OPPORTUNITY.

Part of our calling as followers of Jesus is to engage the world at every opportunity. We are to provide a moral and prophetic voice for the community and for the nation—a voice that, among other things, restrains evil and protects the weak and vulnerable. Unfortunately, in recent decades, the Church, including the evangelical church, has to

some extent compromised its prophetic voice because it has been co-opted by materialism or the hunger for power that comes from associating too closely with a particular political party or movement.

Even though it can be challenging to do so without becoming mixed up in partisan politics, leaders in the church should seek and welcome opportunities to wield influence in the public square. I (John) have had a few chances, beginning during the Jimmy Carter years, to make a bit of a difference at a national level. Under President Carter, I participated in a taskforce that worked closely with Vice President Mondale to address needs in rural poor black communities.

LEADERS IN THE CHURCH SHOULD SEEK AND WELCOME OPPORTUNITIES TO WIELD INFLUENCE IN THE PUBLIC SQUARE.

Years later, at a gathering of about 20 religious leaders, President Clinton asked the group why evangelicals didn't like him. Talk about having to speak truth to power! Though some in the group hedged and came to the president's defense, I explained that many in the evangelical community felt like he didn't care about issues that were important to them. Later in that same meeting, I told President Clinton about a situation I'd heard about in which a church that had accepted some government money to address humanitarian needs had been ordered to take down its cross. Immediately, the president got on the phone, saying he was going to personally see to it that this issue got resolved.

Under President Reagan's administration, I had the opportunity to influence efforts to alleviate hunger in the country. I was part of a nationwide effort that helped, for example, to create food distribution networks and to remove liability from companies for giving away food to organizations serving those in need. During the George H.W. Bush years, I participated in discussions that led to the term "faith-based organizations" coming into vogue. Currently, Noel Castellanos, CEO of

the Christian Community Development Association, serves on President Obama's Council for Faith and Neighborhood Partnerships.

Not everyone has the opportunity to shape public policy on a national or statewide level. However, virtually all of us can influence public policy at the local or community level—which, most would agree, is ultimately more significant in terms of affecting how people live from day to day.

Jesus once likened His followers to salt (see Matt. 5:13). Salt is a preservative. By making this comparison, Jesus gave the Church the assignment to restrain evil and preserve order. We are called to venture boldly into the public square and be a helpful part of our greater society. We are also called to love those, including our enemies (see Matt. 5:44), whom we encounter as we do so.

Changing public policy is high on the list of priorities for the Christian Community Development Association. We encourage people not to retreat from society, but to engage in the world around them. Each annual CCDA conference includes workshops that have public policy implications, focusing on topics such as immigration and education reform, the juvenile justice system, and institutional racism.

VIRTUALLY ALL OF US CAN INFLUENCE PUBLIC POLICY AT THE LOCAL OR COMMUNITY LEVEL—WHICH IS ULTIMATELY MORE SIGNIFICANT IN TERMS OF AFFECTING HOW PEOPLE LIVE FROM DAY TO DAY.

Confronting the powers and principalities of the world is not nearly so dangerous for U.S. Christians as it is in other parts of the world—or as it was at various points in our own history. Many older people still remember the days when black people faced physical and economic consequences simply for registering (or trying to register) to vote. A peaceful march from Selma, Alabama, to Montgomery in 1965 resulted in "Bloody Sunday," in which some 600 civil rights demonstrators were attacked at the Edmund Pettus Bridge by police

officers using tear gas and clubs. That sacrifice went a long way toward giving African Americans the right to vote.

Whether we face the threat of violence or simply the possibility that people will reject what we say, it's important for the Church to embrace its mission of offering a prophetic voice to society—a voice that represents biblical values within the social and political structures of our world. Remember that we are not advocating siding with a particular political party. Christian values are not exclusively Democratic, Republican, Libertarian or anything else. We have a responsibility to affirm or challenge efforts and initiatives based on their own merit, not on support for a political party, some of whose goals may not be consistent with biblical values. The best approach is for Christians across the political spectrum to unite around particular initiatives—whether local or national—that seek to solve problems and bring about positive change.

THE CHURCH MUST EMBRACE ITS MISSION OF OFFERING A PROPHETIC VOICE TO SOCIETY—A VOICE THAT REPRESENTS BIBLICAL VALUES WITHIN THE SOCIAL AND POLITICAL STRUCTURES OF OUR WORLD.

For most leaders, the greatest opportunities for influence will not be national, but local—which, as we already noted, are the most important opportunities anyway. Former House Speaker Tip O'Neill was right when he coined the phrase "All politics is local." Local policies have a direct effect on community members' lives, so it's strategic for leaders to show up at school board and city council meetings, and to develop friendships with local community and political leaders. Personally, I (Wayne) feel at least as comfortable operating in so-called secular settings as I do in some Christian settings.

When active in the public square, it's important to be clear about our values and goals, while still being kind and polite, remembering that we are ambassadors for Christ, attempting to shine the light of God wherever we go. One way to represent biblical values is to offer to pray at public meetings. This is something I have done many times.

I've prayed before the Cook County (Chicago) Board of Commissioners and the Illinois legislature. I met with former Chicago mayor Richard Daley several times in his office. I always asked if I could pray and was never refused. Chicago's current mayor, Rahm Emanuel, came to Lawndale to participate in the ribbon cutting for our health and fitness center. This event coincided with a CCDA board meeting. When I brought the mayor in to meet CCDA's leaders, John and our Board Chair, Barbara Williams-Skinner, suggested that we pray for the mayor—and we did. (In fact, I pray for him every morning.)

There is a delicate balance to be maintained between being bold in representing Christian values and remembering that we live in a religiously pluralistic society. When we speak in the public square, there is nothing wrong with making it clear that we speak as Christians. But it makes sense, from both moral and strategic perspectives, to recognize that we will frequently encounter people whose value systems are rooted in other religions or philosophies—and that our religious differences need not prevent us from working together toward shared goals. The fact that some of those who founded our country were Christians does not make the United States a Christian nation. In fact, religious freedom was one of our country's founding principles. Viewed in that light, any effort to impose our religious views on others can be considered un-American.

Respecting those who come from different faith backgrounds entails avoiding "Thus saith the Lord" kinds of pronouncements. We will build much stronger relationships, and have more success in our endeavors, if we are tolerant of other viewpoints and seek opportunities to work with all people to bring healing and justice to our communities. Of course, none of this keeps us from sharing our Christian faith as opportunities and invitations arise.

## A Broader View of the Public Square

The public square encompasses much more than just political issues and public policy. It also includes such realms as public education and the criminal justice system. In fact, making sure that people who have been accused (whether justly or unjustly) have someone to stand by them is one of my (Wayne's) top priorities. If someone from our church

is in the hospital, there's a decent chance I won't go visit that person—though someone from the church certainly will. But if it's a major court case, I make sure to be there.

WHEN DIVERSE COMMUNITY MEMBERS STAND TOGETHER IN A SHOW OF SUPPORT, IT HAS A POSITIVE EFFECT.

I do this largely out of the recognition that most of the people in power in the court system are white, while most of those who have been accused are people of color. Many who have run afoul of the law don't have anyone, even family members, to support them. When I go to court, I try to bring as many other people with me as I can. I want the judge to see that the person whose fate will be determined that day has lots of people—including a white man wearing a suit and tie—who believe in him or her. When diverse community members stand together in a show of support, I'm convinced it has a positive effect.

On one occasion, someone from our church was sent to jail, even though I and others who knew him well had virtually no doubt he was innocent. Bail was set at $50,000—thus he would have to come up with $5,000 to be released. He didn't have this kind of money—and the longer he stayed in jail, the more hours of work he missed, making his financial situation more difficult. I asked the public defender to petition the judge to reduce the bail. The defender assured me that such a petition would fall on deaf ears. I asked her, as a favor, to do it anyway, pointing out that it wouldn't hurt to give it a try. I suggested that she mention to the judge that the accused had dozens of people, including two of his pastors, there to support him.

The public defender finally consented. The state attorney argued strongly against even hearing the petition for reduced bail, let alone granting it. But in the end, the judge lowered the amount to $15,000. Our friend was able to come up with $1,500, and thus was freed and able to go back to work. He was eventually found not guilty, and he's back to work and in church every Sunday.

On another occasion, we organized an effort to prevent the closing of a local hospital. About 1,000 people—children and adults of all ages—formed a human chain around the entire block. It was a completely peaceful event—not so much a protest as a declaration that we needed the hospital in the community. We held hands and prayed. The gathering attracted a few television cameras, and the decision to close the hospital was reversed for a time, although eventually it did close. We have organized other, similar efforts, including taking a few busloads of people to meet with the Chicago Transportation Authority over transportation issues. We make a special effort to include those we are developing as leaders in these kinds of activities, in the hopes that their vision for how the people of God can bring about positive change in the world will be expanded.

## Working with the State

Engaging the world can sometimes mean accepting money from the government or secular foundations. Churches and other faith-based organizations turn to this option partly because there's simply not enough money coming from Christian sources to support the community development work we are trying to do. Virtually all inner-city Christian ministries struggle financially. While much excellent work is done in targeted areas (whether geographical or demographic), the Church of Jesus Christ has not gotten involved in caring for the poor in America in any far-reaching, systematic way.

ENGAGING THE WORLD CAN SOMETIMES MEAN ACCEPTING MONEY FROM THE GOVERNMENT OR SECULAR FOUNDATIONS.

Some Christian organizations have qualms about accepting government money, but we have no problem with using state or federal funds to support ministry. Because Christians are taxpayers, we gave

some of that money to the government in the first place. There are limitations on what Christian ministries can do with the funds they accept, but for the most part we have not found the limitations to be burdensome. It's simply a matter of ensuring compliance with the policies of the funding organization. This typically means that government funds cannot directly support sectarian causes. So, for example, a ministry can use government money to build a medical clinic, but not to purchase Bibles. For a ministry that wants to start a medical clinic to serve its community, that is no burden at all. We can still live as Christians as we interact with those we are serving.

THERE ARE LIMITATIONS ON WHAT CHRISTIAN MINISTRIES CAN DO WITH THE FUNDS THEY ACCEPT, BUT FOR THE MOST PART THE LIMITATIONS ARE NOT BURDENSOME.

At Lawndale, we have on several occasions accepted government money to build affordable housing. By accepting this money, we agree that we will not discriminate with regard to who can live in those houses. This is no burden at all, because we don't want just Christian people to be living in the houses or apartments we build. We don't want to be sheltered from the world, so our housing is open to Muslims, Buddhists, atheists, agnostics, and anyone else who has a need. There is no government regulation stipulating that we can't love all people in the name of Jesus Christ.

Now, it's true that there are times when the strings attached to secular or government funds present ethical issues. On one occasion at Lawndale, we accepted $250,000 to support our medical clinic. Then we found out that, although we would not be required to perform abortions ourselves, we would be required to refer those who wished to terminate their pregnancies to an abortion clinic. The staff and board of the Lawndale Christian Health Center met and decided unanimously to give the money back. We were blessed just a few weeks later with

$100,000 from the same funding source to support abstinence counseling in public schools.

Christian ministries should always be careful not to let donors (funding sources) dictate their vision. It's critical that we know exactly who we are—not just with regard to values and principles, but also with respect to what we are called to do and what we are capable of doing well. This forethought must take place before deciding to pursue or accept funding from secular or government sources—or anyone else.

At Lawndale, we have people who, as part of their job description, look for funding sources to support our multimillion-dollar operation. But we try to limit to 10 percent what we take from any one source, and under no circumstances will we go above 20 percent. Maintaining this balance in our funding sources makes it less likely that we will feel pressure to conform to a funder's vision of what we should be about rather than remaining true to our own.

In sum, the Church should not be cloistered. It has always been meant to engage the world. As we develop leaders for the revolution, we want to raise up people who will not be fearful of living in and confronting the world—and at the same time loving the world—just as Jesus did. There is absolutely no reason to be afraid of the world, because when we walk in the world we do so in the power of Christ and the Holy Spirit—and we have the assurance that "the one who is in [us] is greater than the one who is in the world" (1 John 4:4).

CHAPTER TWELVE

# A PROGRAMMATIC APPROACH TO DEVELOPING LEADERS

Much of leadership development happens spontaneously and informally. As we have mentioned, those we are developing often aren't even aware that this is what we are doing. But there is also a place for a more overt, formal, programmatic approach to developing leaders. Just as people would take a computer class to learn more about computer programs or an art class to learn more about art, so too those who want to be leaders can gain valuable information and skills through a class on leadership.

MUCH OF LEADERSHIP DEVELOPMENT HAPPENS SPONTANEOUSLY AND INFORMALLY. BUT THERE IS A PLACE FOR A MORE OVERT, FORMAL, PROGRAMMATIC APPROACH TO DEVELOPING LEADERS.

Like other classes, a structured leadership course would include assigned readings, lecture and discussion, and opportunities for hands-on experience. At Lawndale, we have offered a leadership class that specifically seeks to develop indigenous leaders—not just in terms of their knowledge and skills, but also with regard to their confidence in their ability to lead. In the pages that follow, we will offer a detailed description of that class; we hope that other churches and ministries will consider what we did at Lawndale as a model, any or all of which can be modified and adapted to fit a variety of contexts.

I (Wayne) led the leadership development class at Lawndale. We invited nearly three-dozen people—all of whom were already leading at some level—to participate. All board members and heads of church ministries were among the invitees. In the end, 15 people—most of them lifelong residents of Lawndale—completed the class. Our time together as a group totaled about 70 hours over the course of 10 months. The class met three times a month on Wednesday nights from 7 to 9 P.M. We sat around an oval table, which enabled everyone to have good eye contact with everyone else. In addition to the 30 2-hour sessions, we spent 8 hours together on a Saturday retreat.

Those participating were expected to attend all classes and related activities, as well as to arrive on time and to participate in class discussions. They were expected to spend an equal amount of time outside of class doing homework. They were also required to create and complete a project—such as a seminar or a program—that would enable them to practice the leadership principles they were learning. This class was not easy. Among other things, I wanted to get across the message that leadership involves responsibility. Those who aspire to lead will be called upon to make commitments and to work hard to fulfill them.

## Class Content and Structure

The content of the class was built around seven basic elements of Christian leadership:

1. Qualities of Leadership
2. Skills for Leading
3. Secrets of Leadership
4. Christian Character
5. Cultural and Environmental Factors
6. Mentoring
7. Leadership Experience

The textbooks we selected covered five of these seven components. To address the qualities of a leader, we used John Maxwell's *The 21 Indispensable Qualities of a Leader*. Not only does this book provide an analysis of 21 attributes of a leader, but it also includes practical exercises to develop each quality.

To improve leadership skills, we chose *The 7 Habits of Highly Effective People*, by Stephen Covey. This book helped participants to improve in areas such as time management and clearly defining one's purpose. Each of the 7 habits represents a valuable leadership skill. For the Secrets of Leadership component, we used Maxwell's *The 21 Irrefutable Laws of Leadership*, which lays out formulas for successful leadership.

We used Dr. Jawanza Kunjufu's *Restoring the Village, Values, and Commitments* to address the Cultural and Environmental Factors component. In this book, Dr. Kunjufu addresses many of the environmental

and cultural factors that have stood as barriers to leadership development in low-income African-American communities like North Lawndale. Finally, we used the Bible in every class session as a foundational text for teaching Christian character.

JAMES 1:19 SAYS, "EVERYONE SHOULD BE QUICK TO LISTEN, SLOW TO SPEAK AND SLOW TO BECOME ANGRY." NOT SURPRISINGLY, GOOD LEADERS ARE GOOD LISTENERS.

Each of the 30 class sessions was divided into seven segments, corresponding to the seven components of leadership. Participants arrived having read the assigned sections from the textbooks. We began each class with a focus on Christian character as we read a portion of Scripture that had special relevance for leadership. The reading was followed by a brief (5 to 10 minutes) teaching on the passage and then class discussion.

It's not hard to find Scripture passages that support the goal of becoming better leaders. Among the passages we unpacked as a class was James 1:19: "My dear brothers, take note of this: Everyone should be quick to listen, slow to speak and slow to become angry." Not surprisingly, we used this verse to emphasize that good leaders are good listeners.

The Christian character segment also included a focus on personal spiritual renewal, rooted in a daily quiet time. One session was devoted to a particular aspect of daily devotions: journaling. Each student was asked to make a copy of two journal entries that he or she felt comfortable sharing, and to turn these in. I read them and gave feedback.

Typically, the segment on Christian character was followed by a 20-minute discussion on one of the "Laws of Leadership," such as the "Law of Priorities" or the "Law of Sacrifice." Each session also included a discussion of a particular leadership skill, such as the skill of beginning with the end in mind (which entails having a purpose). I guided students in

crafting personal mission statements as well as job, ministry or family mission statements. This took place over the course of several weeks.

Other leadership skills we discussed included time management, interpersonal relationships, and win/win problem solving. Also, in each class session we addressed at least one cultural or environmental factor that influences leadership in some way.

One very practical skill the students worked on was public speaking. Several in the class had never given a public speech. After learning the basic elements that go into a speech, each student had an opportunity to present a short speech to the class. Students also had opportunities over the 10 months to lead class discussions.

The class included a strong mentoring element. It was not possible for me to mentor 15 people one on one. I did, however, begin each class by looking the students in the eye and saying, "You are a leader." Inasmuch as a person's self-image influences his or her ability to lead, I wanted to make sure they felt affirmed as current and future leaders.

INASMUCH AS A PERSON'S SELF-IMAGE INFLUENCES HIS OR HER ABILITY TO LEAD, IT IS IMPORTANT TO MAKE SURE THEY FEEL AFFIRMED AS CURRENT AND FUTURE LEADERS.

Students also had the opportunity to observe the process of designing and carrying out a particular ministry activity. In this case, it was a men's prayer walk. This walk consisted of a group of men from the church walking around the neighborhood and stopping at every corner to pray. The event involved careful planning and preparation, including some basic training on how to interact with people we might meet along the way. Women from the church prayed for us as we left, and they remained at the church while we were gone. We gathered for a time of fellowship and thanksgiving afterwards. But the important thing, for the purposes of the leadership class, was that students got to see from the beginning how everything unfolded.

The class included a strong emphasis on hands-on experience, because people grow as leaders largely as a result of being given opportunities to lead. As noted earlier, students practiced leadership skills during class by leading discussions. In addition, each student had to carry out a project in which he or she exercised leadership. The project required a mission statement. Using volunteers was also mandatory, as was a report on the project assessing its effectiveness.

HANDS-ON EXPERIENCE IS VITAL BECAUSE PEOPLE GROW AS LEADERS AS A RESULT OF BEING GIVEN OPPORTUNITIES TO LEAD.

Drew Goldsmith was among those who took the leadership development class. Using skills he had learned in the class, he and his wife, Toya, developed a vision to close down a portion of Ogden Avenue (a major thoroughfare otherwise known as Route 66) for an entire day in order to stage a classic and antique car show. This has become an extremely popular annual community event. Ogden is closed from 7 A.M. until 6 P.M. one Sunday each September. The event includes an outdoor church service attended by thousands—including many men who might not otherwise attend church events but are drawn in by the classic cars. In large part as a result of his work on this event, Drew has emerged as a major leader in our community.

At the end of the 10 months, each student was challenged to commit to mentoring a younger person for at least a year, and those who agreed to take the challenge signed a leadership-mentoring covenant to demonstrate their commitment.

## Assessing Success

Assessing any class or program you hold will help you learn what to do differently the next time (as well as what to keep). It will also likely be a source of encouragement to students, who will have the opportunity to see for themselves how much they have grown as leaders.

Students in the Lawndale class completed a leadership skills inventory prior to the class. The inventory was developed by Terry Anderson and appears in his book *Transforming Leadership*. It covers a total of 56 skills, divided into 5 categories: personal mastery; interpersonal communication; counseling and problem management; team and organizational development; and versatility in style, role, and skill-shifting.[1] This pre-class inventory enabled the students to focus on those areas where they felt they had the most room for growth.

In addition to the inventory, students were asked four questions prior to beginning the class: (1) Where are you presently exercising leadership? (2) What are your spiritual gifts as you perceive them? (3) What are your primary talents and skills? and (4) On a scale of 1 to 10, with 10 being the highest, how do you rate your effectiveness as a leader?

After completing the class, students took the same skills inventory, and thus were able to see for themselves how much, based on their own assessment, they had grown as leaders with respect to particular skills.

A FORMAL LEADERSHIP CLASS PRESENTS AN OPPORTUNITY FOR LEADERS TO BUILD THEIR LIVES INTO THOSE THEY ARE DEVELOPING IN A FOCUSED AND INTENTIONAL WAY.

Upon the completion of the class, we held a celebration dinner at which we reflected on what we had experienced and learned. A post-class survey consisted of the following questions: (1) What did you learn in class that was most helpful to you as a leader? (2) What lesson did you learn that has helped you in your leadership role? (3) Are you a better leader because of this class? and (4) Would you recommend this class to others? Why or why not?

The class produced many positive byproducts. I found it exciting to see people step into leadership roles for the first time or progress to roles involving greater responsibility. One woman who took the class started a ministry that has become extremely well organized and

successful. Working with Prison Fellowship, she put together an Angel Tree Christmas program for children in the Lawndale community whose parents are incarcerated. This program helps more than 700 children have a wonderful Christmas each year.

One of our students went back to school, as the class produced in him a hunger for learning. Another, who at the outset of the class did not see himself as a leader of any kind, began a home repair ministry. He has organized volunteers to come together to help several widows and elderly community members get their homes repaired. In all, the class resulted in 12 new ministries.

A formal class need not and should not replace the leadership development efforts that move forward spontaneously. But it does present an opportunity for leaders to build their lives into those they are developing in a very focused and intentional way. Such efforts are sure to advance the leadership revolution.

**Note**

1. Terry D. Anderson, *Transforming Leadership* (Boca Raton, FL: CRC Press, 1998), pp. 26-36.

CHAPTER THIRTEEN

# DEVELOPING LEADERS FROM THE PULPIT

A Sunday morning message can be a golden opportunity to introduce or reinforce themes that contribute to the development of leaders. The following message is adapted from a sermon I (Wayne) preached at Lawndale Community Church. In addition to illustrating how one can develop leaders through preaching, this message also reinforces many of the ideas that appear throughout this book.

Let me begin by asking a question: Who is your leader? By this I mean: Whom do you follow? Who influences you to do some things and not to do other things? To whom do you listen? The persons you listen to with an eye toward taking their advice are your leaders.

A lot of voices compete for our attention—on television, on the radio, through the Internet, and at our places of work. We have to be careful to whom we listen, whom we follow, and whom we allow to be our leaders.

THE PERSONS YOU LISTEN TO
WITH AN EYE TOWARD TAKING THEIR ADVICE
ARE YOUR LEADERS.

Many of us have the wrong idea about leadership. When we think of a leader, we tend to think of someone who is above us in some way—someone who has an impressive title or a higher spot on the organizational chart. But that's not the best way to define a leader. A lot of people ignore their boss at work but take advice from their parents or maybe their children. So the boss might be a leader on paper but not in reality. Leaders are not necessarily those with titles or positions of authority, although people with titles and authority certainly can be leaders. Leaders are those we listen to and follow, regardless of title or position.

I'm convinced that everyone reading this book is a leader. You might not be a leader of a Fortune 500 company or a school or some political jurisdiction, but you are a leader nonetheless. If someone is listening to you and following you, then you're a leader. A six-year-old

girl may have a four-year-old sibling watching her, which makes her a leader. A six-year-old boy who sees his older brother kick a ball down the street is likely to start kicking the ball in the same way.

Leadership is influence. It's not always good influence. If Mom or Dad lights up a cigarette, guess what little Johnny is likely to be doing someday when no one is looking? I want you to know how significant you are. People are watching you—just as you are watching others. If you are a mother, your children are watching you—which makes you a leader. In fact, mothers just might be the most important leaders on the face of this earth.

So all of us are leaders. The next question is: What kind of leader will you be? Will you be a good leader, a bad leader, or a mediocre leader? Will the influence you have on others be positive, negative or neutral?

Today we are going to focus on a character from the Old Testament: Nehemiah. His story has a lot to teach us about leadership. The Babylonians had taken the Northern Kingdom of Israel into captivity. Jews had to relocate to Babylon (though, as we will see, some remained in Jerusalem during the exile). In 586 BC, the city of Jerusalem was reduced to rubble and the Temple was destroyed. But when the Persians conquered the Babylonians, the Jewish people were allowed to return. Nehemiah, an Israelite who had been serving as an official in the Persian Court, took on the assignment of leading the effort to rebuild the walls around Jerusalem.

I'm going to focus on eight words or phrases, each beginning with the letter *I*, to help us gain some insight into Nehemiah's leadership style and what we can learn from it.

## Inquisitive

The first *I* stands for "inquisitive." Nehemiah asked a lot of questions. Good leaders ask questions so they can better understand the situation—both the challenges they face and the resources they have to work with. Think about it. If you ask someone to lead a particular effort, and that person doesn't ask any questions about the project, you can assume the person isn't really that interested and won't do a very good job.

In the first chapter of the book that bears his name, we find Nehemiah questioning Hanani, whom he identifies as "one of my brothers," about the Jewish remnant that had survived the exile and also about Jerusalem itself (see Neh. 1:2). The "remnant" means those who stayed behind. They never went to Babylon. So they were very familiar with what had happened to Jerusalem and what the conditions were there. Instead of rushing in to get started, Nehemiah began by asking questions. He wanted to know what was really going on.

GOOD LEADERS ASK QUESTIONS SO THEY CAN BETTER UNDERSTAND THE SITUATION—BOTH THE CHALLENGES THEY FACE AND THE RESOURCES THEY HAVE TO WORK WITH.

Sometimes we don't want to know what really happened. We don't want to know how bad a situation might be. The truth can be scary, or it can make us feel overwhelmed. We might hesitate to ask questions because we're not sure we want to hear the answers. But Nehemiah wanted the truth. He wanted to know how bad things were and how difficult the task of rebuilding Jerusalem might be.

Good leaders want facts. They are not interested in rumors, because they know from past experience how often rumors turn out not to be true. Nehemiah consulted eyewitnesses—people who had just come back from Jerusalem and who had seen with their own eyes what was going on there. Sometimes it takes awhile to discover the facts. It takes a little work, and it might keep us from moving as quickly as we want to move. But that's what good leaders do.

## Impacted Deeply

The second *I* stands for "impacted deeply." Leaders are affected in a significant way when they learn of the suffering of others. They identify with the pain of those whom they love. They don't just move on

to the next item of business, as if nothing had happened. They don't run from other people's problems or try to get away from pain.

Through his questioning, Nehemiah found out that those who had survived the exile were "in great trouble and disgrace" (Neh. 1:3). We read in verse 4: "When I heard these things, I sat down and wept." That's the kind of leader I want to follow. I want someone who—when he or she hears about my hurt or struggle—feels my pain with me. I want to know my leader cares about me.

Nehemiah goes on to say that he mourned for several days. "Mourn" is a powerful word. Mourning goes a lot deeper than crying. It's one thing to shed a few tears and move on. Mourning is more like wailing—struggling with the pain. Nehemiah probably had trouble sleeping at night, because he couldn't get the pain of the people off his mind. If he did sleep, I'm sure the first thing he thought about when he woke up was the people back in Jerusalem.

While his initial period of mourning lasted for a few days, Nehemiah's grieving went on for months. We know this because it was the month of Kislev when Nehemiah first learned about the struggles of the people back in Jerusalem, and it was the month of Nisan, which is three or four months later, when he went before the king (see Neh. 2:1). Nehemiah reports that he had never been sad in the king's presence before, but that time the king could tell something was wrong. He asked Nehemiah, "Why does your face look so sad when you are not ill? This can be nothing but sadness of heart" (Neh. 2:2).

LEADERS ARE AFFECTED IN A SIGNIFICANT WAY WHEN THEY LEARN OF THE SUFFERING OF OTHERS.

Even months after hearing the bad news from Jerusalem, Nehemiah could not hide his grief. The pain of the people affected him deep in his heart; he couldn't shake it. It's appropriate and beneficial for leaders—in fact, for all people—to experience the pain of others

and to allow themselves to mourn. Those who move on from pain too quickly will probably be visited by that pain again. Good leaders share the pain of other people. That was Nehemiah.

## Intercessor

The third *I* stands for "intercessor." Chapter 1, verse 4 reads, "When I heard these things, I sat down and wept. For some days I mourned and fasted and prayed before the God of heaven." We've seen how Nehemiah mourned. He also interceded—he fasted and prayed. Leaders are intercessors. They go before God on behalf of their people.

I am the first to admit that when this ministry was in its infancy, I did not adequately understand or appreciate the importance and power of intercessory prayer. I can still recall a meeting we held back in 1978. A small group from the community had gathered, and we wrote on a chalkboard some ideas for what the community needed. Someone mentioned that people needed a safe place to do their laundry, and they suggested that maybe we could get an old washer and dryer and put them in the back of our storefront church so that people from the neighborhood could come and wash their clothes.

LEADERS ARE INTERCESSORS.
THEY GO BEFORE GOD ON BEHALF
OF THEIR PEOPLE.

I didn't think that was such a good idea. My priority was building a gym. But I wanted to be supportive, so I said, "Let's pray about it." The others didn't know that "let's pray about it" was code for "we're not going to do this." Not knowing the code, the people who were at that meeting took my words seriously. They got down on their knees and asked God to send us a washer and dryer. Sure enough, a couple of weeks later, I got a call from a suburban couple who had heard about our fledgling ministry. They said they had changed the color

scheme of their utility room and wanted to know if we could use a washer and dryer.

I told them that the people of our church and community had been praying for a washer and dryer. But I still wasn't excited about the idea, so I said we appreciated their offer, but we had no way of transporting the appliances to Lawndale. However, the man said he could borrow a truck and bring them himself. Before long—and in spite of my resistance—we had a washer and dryer, and they were both put to work to serve the community.

PRAYER BRINGS GOD'S HELP,
AND GOOD LEADERS KNOW THEY
CAN'T DO IT ON THEIR OWN.

This is a good example of grassroots initiative from the community. It also showed us—showed me—what can happen when we take prayer seriously. The first thing Nehemiah did after being impacted deeply was to fast and pray about the situation: "O LORD, God of heaven, the great and awesome God, who keeps his covenant of love with those who love him and obey his commands" (Neh. 1:5).

Leaders pray for the situation and for their people. Prayer brings God's help, and good leaders know they can't do it on their own.

## Involved

Good leaders also get involved. That's what Nehemiah did. Living in the king's palace, he had a pretty comfortable life. He most likely had a nice bed to sleep in and got three squares a day. But he cared too deeply about those who were struggling not to get involved.

"If it pleases the king and if your servant has found favor in his sight," Nehemiah said, "let him send me to the city in Judah where my fathers are buried so that I can rebuild it" (Neh. 2:5). Nehemiah could have tried to solve the problems of the people back in Jerusalem from a distance.

After explaining to the king why he was sad, he could have asked him to send his army along with some engineers and builders and carpenters to rebuild Jerusalem. But he wanted to get personally involved.

His willingness to get involved doesn't mean that Nehemiah wasn't afraid (see Neh. 2:2). Most, if not all, leaders experience fear from time to time. Sometimes there is fear from knowing that the task ahead is daunting and the path might not always be safe. Sometimes we may have fears about our own shortcomings or inadequacies as leaders. Nehemiah felt fear, but he still committed himself fully to the task and got personally involved.

Some of us are reluctant to get personally involved. We care about other people's problems, but we don't want to get too close to a negative situation. We might get dirty or tired or hurt. We try to ignore the fact that people around the world are crying for others to get involved in their lives—to get involved with their pain and struggle. Newspaper articles sometimes describe a person getting beaten up while a crowd looks on. There might be dozens of people there, but no one gets involved. Everyone wants to keep a safe distance. That's understandable—but it's not what leaders do.

Nehemiah was not as concerned about being safe as he was about getting involved and easing the pain of others. That's a mark of good leaders. They don't leave things up to someone else. They encourage others to get involved by leading the way.

## Investigator

The fifth *I* stands for "investigator." Nehemiah didn't arrive in Jerusalem amid great fanfare and announce how he was going to make everything right. We read in Nehemiah 2:12 that he "set out during the night" with a few others. "I had not told anyone what my God had put in my heart to do for Jerusalem." In verse 13, we read: "By night I went out through the Valley Gate toward the Jackal Wall and the Dung Gate, examining the walls of Jerusalem, which had been broken down, and its gates, which had been destroyed by fire."

Instead of rushing into action, Nehemiah investigated. He assessed the situation. That's what good leaders do. We see some leaders, including politicians, when they have an idea about how to solve a problem,

call a big press conference so they can announce to the world all that they are going to do to solve the problem. Then once the TV cameras are gone, they don't do anything. Or they do something counterproductive, because they didn't do their research, and the problem gets worse.

INSTEAD OF RUSHING INTO ACTION, GOOD LEADERS ASSESS THE SITUATION. THEY GET ALL THE HELP AND INFORMATION THEY CAN FROM OTHERS.

Nehemiah was smarter and more humble than that. He didn't call a press conference to announce his arrival and to claim he had all the answers. In fact, he recognized that he didn't know what to do. He had been away for a while, and he was out of touch. He didn't arrive from the king's palace thinking he had all the answers. He investigated—and he didn't go alone. He took people with him in order to get different opinions and perspectives. We ought to be leery of those who want to be leaders and are so sure they have all the answers that they don't ask anybody else for advice or input. Good leaders get all the help and information they can from others.

Investigating ought to include getting as close to the grassroots as possible. It can certainly be helpful to consult outside experts, but focus on input from community members. One of our most common sayings in CCDA is: "The people with the problem have the best solutions." It's our job as leaders to listen to people and then come alongside and help. That's what Nehemiah did. His approach to leadership reflects his humility.

## Inclusive

The sixth *I* stands for "inclusive." Nehemiah included other people. As already noted, he took others with him to survey the situation. He also included others in the actual rebuilding of the city. Good leaders don't act alone. They don't come up with or carry out plans in isolation. They surround themselves with others—and not just with "yes people" who are always going to agree with them. Former Secretary

of State Colin Powell said he liked to have a "noisy group" of people around him. He wanted people to come and tell him the truth, not just what he wanted to hear. He wanted his office to be filled with a variety of opinions and ideas.

GOOD LEADERS DON'T ACT ALONE. THEY DON'T COME UP WITH OR CARRY OUT PLANS IN ISOLATION.

So did Nehemiah. He realized he couldn't succeed if he acted alone. He needed others to help both in the planning and the execution. The key to Nehemiah's approach can be found in chapter 2, verse 17. He doesn't say, "Come and help me rebuild." He says, "Come, let us rebuild the wall of Jerusalem, and we will no longer be in disgrace." For Nehemiah, it's not about "you helping me." It's about us being in this thing together. Nehemiah is in essence saying, "I can't do this without you, and what's more, I have no desire to do it without you."

I believe that our Lawndale Community Church gym is unique among all the gyms in Chicago—and maybe in the world! There are thousands of gyms in the Chicago area, but to my knowledge ours is the only one whose foundation was dug by hand by kids from the neighborhood. There was a part of me back in those days that wanted to go find some money and rent a Caterpillar and some other machinery to come in here and dig it out in two or three days. But now I'm glad I didn't do that.

You know how kids say the darnedest things? One day our kids said, "The architect says we gotta dig a hole 7 feet deep, 125 feet long, and 50 feet wide." Then they added, "We can do it." So we got some picks and shovels and wheelbarrows, and for 9 months people came here and dug, 6 days a week. Finally, someone donated a Caterpillar, and the job got finished. It took 9 months instead of 2 or 3 days. But the gym has so much meaning for us today because everyone got involved, and we did it together.

## Ingenious

The seventh *I* stands for "ingenious." Nehemiah certainly displayed ingenuity. We learn in chapter 4 that he became aware of substantial opposition to the rebuilding of Jerusalem's walls and gates. The wall was only half as high as it needed to be, and the builders knew a hostile army could attack them at any time. So Nehemiah devised a plan. Half of the workers would carry swords and spears, while the other half worked to rebuild. As for those delivering materials, they carried the supplies with one hand and held a weapon with the other, so they were always prepared to ward off an attack. Nehemiah also kept a man with a trumpet close by; in the event of an attack, the trumpet would sound, and the people would drop everything (except their weapons) and come to help.

GOOD LEADERS DON'T GIVE UP UNTIL THEY FIND WORKABLE SOLUTIONS. THEY DEMONSTRATE THOUGHTFULNESS AND CREATIVITY.

Good leaders are ingenious in how they act. They don't give up until they find workable solutions. In their leadership, they demonstrate thoughtfulness and creativity. These attributes are of course related to some of the others, mainly investigating and inclusivity. The more leaders assess the situation and seek the advice of others, the more creative and ingenious their plans for addressing challenges will be.

## Inspirational

The final *I* stands for "inspirational." Leaders are people who inspire. John Perkins regularly defines leadership in terms of getting people to do things that they don't want to do. That's inspiration; that's leadership. But John goes a step beyond that. He adds that when the people finish doing the thing they didn't want to do, when they look back, they're glad they did it. This suggests that leaders stay with the people throughout the process and continue to encourage and inspire them.

The wall in Jerusalem got to half its height because "the people worked with all their heart" (Neh. 4:6). Leaders inspire people not just to go through the motions, but also to put their whole hearts into the effort. If our hearts are in what we are doing, we can overcome whatever pain and frustration the road to success includes. When I was a high school coach, there were times when the football players or wrestlers were just going through their routines. Their hearts weren't in it. I would blow the whistle, call them in, and explain that they were never going to improve if their hearts weren't in it.

LEADERS INSPIRE PEOPLE NOT JUST TO GO THROUGH THE MOTIONS, BUT ALSO TO PUT THEIR WHOLE HEARTS INTO THE EFFORT.

Often the hardest time to press on is when a job is half done. We're tired from what we've done, and we're overwhelmed by how much more there still is to do. In Nehemiah's situation, on top of everything else, the people were getting word about possible attacks from the outside. But leaders don't give up. They know how to inspire. When times are toughest, they help people keep their eyes on the prize—focusing on the future hope, not the present reality. They pat people on the back, look them in the eye, and say, "You did a good job today." When people think they can't do any more, leaders say, "I know you can do it."

I can imagine Nehemiah walking along the wall to see how everyone was doing. I can imagine him learning the names of the workers one day, and then coming back the next day and saying, "Joseph, I can see you got a little bit more done today. Benjamin, keep up the good work." He'd call them by name. He might shake their hands or give them high fives. Then he'd take his turn working with them—getting his hands dirty while doing his part to build the wall. As we've said, leaders walk alongside, sharing the pain and struggle. This, in and of itself, serves to inspire.

So we see that Nehemiah was inquisitive. He was sensitive, impacted deeply by the pain and struggles of those around him. He was an intercessor; he prayed for those he loved. He didn't try to solve problems from a distance. He got personally involved. Instead of moving forward as if he had all the answers, he investigated the situation, and he included others both in the planning and the work itself. He used his ingenuity to devise creative solutions to problems. And he was inspirational; he found ways to make sure the people had their whole hearts in the work they were doing.

Nehemiah is an example of the kind of leader I want to be. I hope and believe that's the kind of leader you want to be, too. Shall we pray? *Lord Jesus, help us. We've learned that every one of us, from the youngest to the oldest, is a leader if somebody's following us—if we have some influence over somebody. Lord, we pray to become more like Nehemiah—to develop the traits of a Christian leader. We ask Your special help in this. I pray for each person here that You would help them to become better leaders, modeled after Nehemiah and shaped by Your Word. Help us, Lord, to lead in a godly fashion. We pray this in Your name, Jesus. Amen.*

CHAPTER FOURTEEN

# LEADERSHIP LESSONS FROM MOSES

Over the years, I (John) have preached or spoken on the topic of Moses and leadership many times. This chapter is a collection of some of my teachings on Moses as it relates to themes advanced in this book.

Moses' story spans four entire books in the Old Testament, beginning with the story of his birth in the second chapter of Exodus and ending with the account of his death in the final chapter of Deuteronomy. However, the easiest way to get a summary of the life of Moses is to read a mere seven verses in the New Testament book of Hebrews:

> By faith Moses' parents hid him for three months after he was born, because they saw he was no ordinary child, and they were not afraid of the king's edict.
>
> By faith Moses, when he had grown up, refused to be known as the son of Pharaoh's daughter. He chose to be mistreated along with the people of God rather than to enjoy the pleasures of sin for a short time. He regarded disgrace for the sake of Christ as of greater value than the treasures of Egypt, because he was looking ahead to his reward. By faith he left Egypt, not fearing the king's anger; he persevered because he saw him who is invisible. By faith he kept the Passover and the sprinkling of blood, so that the destroyer of the firstborn would not touch the firstborn of Israel.
>
> By faith the people passed through the Red Sea as on dry land; but when the Egyptians tried to do so, they were drowned (Heb. 11:23-29).

If we take a close look at the circumstances surrounding the life of Moses—and at his actions—we'll find there is a lot to learn about leadership.

## No Excuses

If anyone had a reason to make excuses for not succeeding—for not being the best he could be—it was Moses. He was born in poverty as a slave. In fact, he was supposed to be killed the moment he was born. His mother had to abandon him in order to save his life. What kind of psychological damage must that have done?

But Moses did not allow a troubled past to keep him down. He did not make excuses. Too many people today wrongly blame their failing present on their difficult past. It's understandable that this would happen among black folk, given our horrific history in this country—and the pain of a tragic past is not limited to black people. Many, many people, for a variety of reasons, have had pasts they would just as soon forget.

UNDERSTANDING HELPS US TO ADDRESS THE PROBLEM, SOLVE IT, AND THEN MOVE ON.

However, the key to success is not to forget, but to remember and to understand. Once we understand why we are who we are, and why we feel as we feel, we can do something about it. That last part is important; the ultimate goal is not just to understand our pasts. Understanding helps us to address the problem, solve it, and then move on.

Moses made a choice not to live out his life as a victim. Had he done so, he would never have become the leader he eventually became. We need to take this same approach. No matter how badly the past has treated us, we can choose not to live as victims. No past should ever disqualify someone from becoming a leader. In fact, one can make the case that leadership qualities emerge as a result of suffering and pain. Thus, James can write, "Consider it pure joy, my brothers, whenever you face trials of many kinds" (Jas. 1:2). This is a crucial message for leaders to get across to those they are developing.

## The Importance of Family

After Moses was born, his parents protected him by hiding him. Yes, he got off to a rough start, but at least he had parents who cared about him. He had a family. God is a communal God—a God of family. That, in part, is the significance of the Trinity: Jesus is the eternal Son within the family of God.

According to God's design, we are created to live and function as part of a larger whole—a family. The breakdown of the family is at the heart of the problems we experience as a society and the challenges we face as Christian leaders today. Children need nurturing. They need a father. They need a mother. They need aunts and uncles and grandparents to love them. They need the security of knowing that they are surrounded by people who care about them and support them.

THE BREAKDOWN OF THE FAMILY IS AT THE HEART OF THE CHALLENGES WE FACE AS CHRISTIAN LEADERS TODAY.

The confidence and sense of security characteristic of leaders are nurtured best in the context of a stable family. So the effort to develop future leaders must include ministry efforts and public policy initiatives designed to strengthen families.

When it comes to family, we as leaders need to make sure our priorities are in the right place. I recall one occasion when we held a Christian Community Development Association board meeting at a location within walking distance of my house. I had to go to my house to get something; my plan was to return to the meeting right away to hear an important message. After all, I was the leader of CCDA. The people would likely wait until I got back to begin the presentation.

As soon as I got home, however, Vera Mae handed me a bicycle with two flats. My granddaughter asked me, "Grandpa, will you fix my bike?"

My first thought was, *I ain't got time for this.*

She asked again, "Will you fix my bike, Grandpa?"

I thought about it some more and then said, "Sure. They can wait. I'm going to fix this bike right now." In a few minutes, my granddaughter was happily riding her bike. That was one of the best leadership decisions I've ever made, because leadership requires understanding priorities—knowing what things can wait and what things are truly important. That day, the message I communicated to my granddaughter

was: "You know, you're the most important person in the world to me right now."

Not everyone has the advantage of coming from a stable, loving family. As Christian leaders and developers of leaders, we will often be required to stand in the gap—to become family to those who have none. By God's grace, people can overcome the deficiencies of the past. Our role is to support them and to never give up on them.

## The Priority of Faith

Notice how often it's mentioned in the passage from Hebrews that Moses' parents and Moses himself were motivated by faith. Moses was nurtured in faith. He spent his early years in a priestly family, where he learned the traditions of his faith, hearing the stories of his ancestors, including Abraham, Isaac and Jacob.

Sometimes we get so caught up in serving others and helping them deal with their external circumstances that we forget the importance of passing on our faith. Faith comes by hearing the Word of God. It's the responsibility of leaders to pass on our faith to our children and to all those who come under our leadership. It's our role also to make sure that our faith plays a part in all we do, from the way we do our jobs to the public policies we support or oppose.

## Nurturing Purpose

As we read Moses' story, it's clear that God had a purpose for his life from the very beginning. Those around him didn't always know it, and Moses probably didn't know it at first, but God knew that this man Moses would play a crucial role in world history. He would lead an entire race of people to a new place after hundreds of years in captivity. Each experience he had in life prepared him for his purpose.

Moses is not alone in having a purpose in life. Each of us also has a purpose—a calling from God. It might not seem as monumental as Moses' purpose, but in God's eyes it's equally significant. Part of the role of a leader is to help people to find their purpose—their calling—and then to nurture it. We do this by creating an environment in which purpose can be realized—an environment in which people are encouraged

to seek their purpose and where they have the freedom and the opportunity to exercise their gifts and skills.

## Demonstrating Courage

Some people wrongly define "courage" as the absence of fear. A better understanding of courage is to say that it is the commitment to press on in spite of fear. It's acting on our convictions—not backing off or caving in—even in the face of danger. That's exactly what leaders sometimes have to do.

Moses demonstrated courage at many points throughout his life—including, as a youth, coming to the defense of one of his Hebrew brethren who was being beaten by an Egyptian. Of course, his most courageous act was going before Pharaoh to ask him to let the Hebrew people go. It's hard to imagine how terrifying this must have been for Moses, even though he knew it was God's will. Moses' objections to being chosen by God (for example, pointing out that he didn't speak well enough to do the job) testify to his reservations—to his fear. But in the end, he obeyed God in spite of his fear.

COURAGE IS ACTING ON OUR CONVICTIONS—NOT BACKING OFF OR CAVING IN—EVEN IN THE FACE OF DANGER.

Courage almost always entails someone doing, in the midst of fear and danger, what he or she has been taught and trained to do. In some cases, we might not recognize the ways God has been preparing us for something until it's time for us to act. This may have been the case with Moses, who spent 40 years in the desert tending his father-in-law's sheep before God called him to lead the people of Israel. Whether Moses realized it or not, God used the experiences of that season to prepare him for the purpose He had assigned to him—and when the time came, Moses did what he had been prepared to do.

I'm reminded of a more contemporary figure, Chesley Sullenberger, who is widely regarded as a hero for successfully landing an airplane on the Hudson River in January 2009, saving all 155 people who were aboard the disabled plane. Certainly he must have been afraid. But he didn't let his fears defeat him or dominate the situation. He managed his fears, harkened back to his training, and calmly and confidently did what he had been prepared to do. That year, Sullenberger ranked second in *Time* magazine's top 100 influential heroes and icons. Was he a hero? Or was he simply doing what he had been taught? Or both?

IN SPITE OF FEAR, LEADERS
DO WHAT THEY'VE BEEN CALLED TO DO
AND PREPARED TO DO.

Leaders don't shy away from difficult circumstances or hard decisions. In spite of fear, they do what they've been called to do and prepared to do.

## Claiming an Identity

Moses was raised in Pharaoh's household and educated at the best schools in Egypt. He talked like an Egyptian. He ate the food Egyptians ate. He dressed like an Egyptian. He was training to be the next pharaoh. But deep down in his heart, Moses knew who he was—he was a Jew. The Bible tells us that Moses refused to be called the son of Pharaoh's daughter (see Heb. 11:24).

As leaders, we need to encourage people to claim their identity and their dignity—to be proud of who they are. This is especially important when ministering among those who for one reason or another lack self-esteem. One of the greatest challenges of the civil rights movement was getting black people to move beyond self-hatred. In fact, this was the greatest challenge. It was one thing for people in power to hate us, to treat us as inferior beings, and to call us "niggers." It was far more damaging when we thought these things about ourselves.

The deepest damage done to black people as a result of racism in this country was the creation of this dynamic of self-hatred. Too many people came to believe they were nobody. Until this was addressed and overcome, the civil rights movement had no chance of making any real progress. It wasn't until people such as Malcolm X and Stokely Carmichael started proclaiming the message that "black is beautiful" that black people began to reclaim their dignity and develop pride in their identity. Truth be told, this is something that many African Americans continue to struggle with today.

AS LEADERS, WE NEED TO ENCOURAGE PEOPLE TO CLAIM THEIR IDENTITY AND THEIR DIGNITY—TO BE PROUD OF WHO THEY ARE.

God wants African-American people to be proud of who they are. He wants Asian people to be proud that they are Asian. He wants Latino people to be proud of their Latin identity. Some churches will be multiethnic, while others will be predominantly one race or another. We can all be proud of who we are while being open to understanding and to seeing the pain and suffering of members of other ethnic groups. We can be who we are and at the same time learn from those who are different.

We need to get beyond anyone feeling they have to apologize for who they are and instead learn to celebrate our diversity and to praise God for His creativity. This is what God wants His Church to be. We are all ultimately one in Christ—equal partners in the family of God.

## Openness to Vision

People debate whether leaders are born or made. I'm not sure how helpful that discussion is. The more important consideration is whether or not people are open to God's vision and calling on their lives. Leaders, like Moses, meet God somewhere—whether on a mountain or in

a quiet living room. They get a vision—an awareness that God has put them in a particular place at a particular time to accomplish a particular mission. Because He's called them to do whatever this thing is, they have no choice but to do it, regardless of their fears and no matter how painful the road ahead might be. All fear and uncertainty are overcome by a feeling of serenity that they are responding to God's call.

For me, this moment came during the civil rights movement at a time when my life and the lives of my family members were at risk. After returning to Mississippi from California, Vera Mae and I had gotten involved with voter registration activities in the Mendenhall area. This didn't sit well with some of the local white folks. We started getting threatening phone calls, and cars started showing up at night—driving real slow past our house. When I shared all of this with some of my neighbors, the community jumped into action. Almost a hundred men arrived each night to protect my house. These men had been dreaming and longing for someone to come and lead them—and they saw something in me (maybe they caught a glimpse of my openness to God's will for my life) that made them think I was that leader. They told me to go to bed and get some rest. "We'll protect you and your family," they said to me. "You are here to do what we can't do, and it's our task to protect you." That's when I knew that God had called me to lead in that situation. I loved and respected these men, and they respected me and loved me dearly. My calling could not have been clearer.

Recognizing and embracing a vision from God creates passion, and passion creates energy. It's important for leaders to learn how to manage this energy. One important aspect of energy management is identifying and using the skills and the intelligence around you. Listen to what people say and observe what they do, so that you can identify skills and talents. Then put those skills to work. It's part of the job of a leader to search for gifts and skills. When I'm with people, I'm listening for talent, looking for gifts, and inviting people to be open to the vision God has for them.

## Humility

As many things as there are to learn from Moses' positive example, there is also an important lesson to learn from his negative example. God denying Moses entry into the Promised Land—after all the dangers

he faced, the times he trusted God, and all those years in the wilderness—is widely viewed as one of the Old Testament's most tragic stories. In Numbers 20, we find the people of Israel complaining that they had no water. God instructed Moses and his brother, Aaron, to "speak to that rock before their eyes and it will pour out its water" (v. 8). But instead of speaking to the rock, Moses, after expressing his frustration with the people, struck the rock twice. The Lord then said to Moses, "Because you did not trust in me enough to honor me as holy in the sight of the Israelites, you will not bring this community into the land I give them" (v. 12).

NO MATTER HOW SUCCESSFUL A LEADER BECOMES, HE OR SHE NEVER GETS TOO BIG FOR GOD.

Scholars have speculated as to exactly what Moses did to deserve so severe a punishment. Was it because he didn't listen to what God had told him to do? Or was it because he got angry? Though we may not understand the details or the cultural dynamics completely, Moses clearly did something to dishonor God in the sight of the people.

The details are not as important as the lesson leaders need to take from this account. It's a lesson in humility. No matter how successful a leader becomes, he or she never gets too big for God. For their own good, God will find a way to bring people back down to where they belong.

It's easy for people to be humble in the beginning, as they labor along in anonymity trying to make ends meet. The game changes when people gain a certain amount of notoriety and perhaps the income to go with it. We've seen it happen countless times to pastors and other leaders. At some point, they forget their roots and start behaving as if they've grown too big for God. Moses' story reminds us that, no matter how significant our accomplishments have been, we never outgrow the need to depend on God and to do things God's way. If we forget this, we might have to learn a lesson the hard way. Thus it becomes important for leaders to reflect regularly on their be-

ginnings—their roots—and to take precautions to ensure that accomplishments and recognition do not take a toll on humility.

Moses is far from alone when it comes to Old Testament characters who, plain and simple, messed up. David, humble in the beginning, eventually thought he could do anything he wanted to do simply because he was king. He was wrong. Let's learn from these examples, keeping in mind that we are saved and we grow not as a result of our goodness, but because of God's grace. This truth is essential for leaders to remember and reflect upon at every turn.

CHAPTER FIFTEEN

# MISCELLANEOUS ADVICE

In our work with CCDA, we have the opportunity to visit other churches, most of them urban, around the country. On some of these visits, many years ago now, we began to take note of the slogans these churches had adopted for their bulletins or signage. We noticed phrases such as "Loving God and Loving Our People" or "Loving God, Loving Our Neighbor." At some point, it occurred to us that, given the similarities to our own motto, other churches might be looking to us a model.

I (Wayne) am still humbled and encouraged every time a church or other organization considers Lawndale Community Church to be a model for pursuing community development from a Christian perspective. We are far from perfect, but God has done amazing work in our midst, and we have learned many valuable lessons over our years of ministry. We are happy to share those lessons and some of our stories with visitors from around the country (and sometimes from other parts of the world) who want to do in their own contexts what we have been doing in Chicago. Following are a few of the things we have learned. We hope that these bits of advice will be helpful to those thinking about starting leadership development ministries as well as to those looking for guidance about issues that leaders tend to face on an ongoing basis.

## "Slow Down"

Among the questions we are asked from time to time is: "What would you do differently if you could turn back the clock?" Of course, when it comes to hundreds of individual situations and challenges we have dealt with over the last few decades, there are many things we'd do differently. But in terms of general advice that we hope others will take to heart, our first offering can be summarized in two words: "Slow down."

It's often the case that a person's weaknesses are in fact strengths taken too far. For example, good leaders are frequently what we might call driven individuals; they are energetic people who are focused on getting things done and getting them done as efficiently as possible. But there are risks associated with working hard and moving fast. Quicker is not always better, and, as discussed earlier, working too hard and too long can become a liability to ourselves and to

our families and friends. African and African-American cultures have much to offer in this regard. They teach us to slow down—to sit, recline, relax, and take it all in instead of constantly thinking about what comes next.

QUICKER IS NOT ALWAYS BETTER, AND WORKING TOO HARD AND TOO LONG CAN BECOME A LIABILITY TO OURSELVES AND TO OUR FAMILIES AND FRIENDS.

Successful leadership is about more than getting things done quickly and efficiently. Ministry, including the ministry of leadership development, is a marathon, not a sprint. Slowing down doesn't mean we are any less passionate about or committed to what we are doing. It simply means we are taking opportunities to live in the moment, to see glimpses of the final outcome before we fully arrive, and to celebrate times of success even amid times of challenge and frustration. Part of slowing down is focusing on obedience and perseverance instead of worrying about results.

## Vision Casting

Casting a vision is a task commonly associated with leadership. Sometimes a leader has a clear vision of a problem and what it will take to solve it. In these cases, what is required is often too big for one person, so the leader recruits, inspires and equips others to follow, so that the vision can be realized. Martin Luther King Jr. had a dream. But the success of that dream would depend on countless others who were inspired by his example and his leadership, and who were willing to make the necessary sacrifices in pursuit of the vision.

A leader, however, need not be someone with his or her own personal vision or an expert at vision casting. He or she can be a facilitator—someone who listens and guides people in developing a vision for their church or community. Vision can be—and perhaps in many

cases *ought* to be—the product of a process that includes prayer, listening, dialogue and careful thinking.

Bill Hybels, the senior pastor at Willow Creek Community Church, is widely regarded as one of the Church's best leadership minds. He has helped countless church leaders over the years through various conferences and events offered by the Willow Creek Association, which he founded. At his leadership summits, never does he say, "God told me." He never personalizes vision. Instead, vision casting is all about facilitating. It's not the product of any particular individual, but of the Church, which is God's vehicle to accomplish the work of the Kingdom until Christ's return.

THE CHURCH IS THE COMMUNITY OF GOD'S PEOPLE. IT'S NOT A PLACE TO IDOLIZE INDIVIDUALS AND PLACE THEM ON PEDESTALS.

In fact, we are wise to be wary of those who talk about what God told them to do. This kind of language has the potential to fuel a cult mentality. The Church is the community of God's people. It's not a place to idolize individuals and place them on pedestals. The scriptural concept of vision has to do with seeing what God sees in relationship to the pain and the problems of God's people. In the Old Testament, God consistently summoned prophets to challenge leaders who ignored the suffering and struggles of the people.

We should be careful not to glamorize or spiritualize vision. By and large, vision has already been revealed to us through Scripture, and there's nothing particularly mystical about it. The Church's purpose is always to share the good news of salvation in Christ, to strive for justice, and to come to the aid of the poor and disenfranchised. How this overarching vision is translated into specific contexts will vary. And this does not negate the possibility of individuals receiving specific visions from God. But any such revealed vision should be examined to ensure that it conforms to scriptural principles and to the voices of the community.

## Highlight Your Mission and Vision

It's important for every church to have a clear understanding of its purpose(s), its mission, and its vision, and to capture this understanding in documents or statements that reflect the church's main goals and describe what sets it apart from other churches. A listing of purposes would address the question, Why are we here? Since its inception, Lawndale Community Church has held to the following four purposes: (1) to reach the unchurched people of the community; (2) to proclaim and live out biblical Christianity; (3) to raise up new generations of Christian leadership; and (4) to creatively meet the needs of people, striving to empower them along the way.

A mission statement emerges from the purposes and should be as focused and concise as possible. Lawndale's reads as follows: "Lawndale Community Church's mission is to redeem the 'Lawndale Community.' The church seeks to bring Christian wholistic revitalization to the lives and environment of its residents through economic empowerment, housing improvement, educational enrichment, quality affordable health care, and Christian discipleship."

A MISSION STATEMENT EMERGES FROM THE PURPOSES OF A CHURCH AND SHOULD BE AS FOCUSED AND CONCISE AS POSSIBLE.

It's helpful if a church's mission can also be captured in a brief slogan. Ideally, every single person who has been a part of your church or ministry for more than a week or two will be able to recite at least your slogan, if not the full mission statement. Our slogan at Lawndale consists of just four words: "Loving God, Loving People." We do our best to make sure this slogan appears in as many places as possible: the church's website, bulletins, the newsletter, advertisements, signage, and more. We reinforce our mission during sermons and at church meetings.

To go along with the mission statement, we recommend that, just as some individuals have life verses, churches adopt purpose verses or passages. At Lawndale, we have taken Matthew 22:34-39 as ours:

> Hearing that Jesus had silenced the Sadducees, the Pharisees got together. One of them, an expert in the law, tested him with this question: "Teacher, which is the greatest commandment in the Law?" Jesus replied: "'Love the Lord your God with all your heart and with all your soul and with all your mind.' This is the first and greatest commandment. And the second is like it: 'Love your neighbor as yourself.'"

We also have a vision statement—something that captures, based on the pursuit of our mission, what we envision the future to be. One might say that the vision statement is what we hope will result from the accomplishment of the mission. Lawndale's vision statement reads as follows: "Lawndale Community Church envisions a future when Christian values undergird the attitudes and actions of Lawndale residents; when existing community people are empowered to live in harmony and security; when vacant lots and abandoned buildings are converted into new, affordable homes and rehabbed apartments; when the majority of homes are owner occupied; when high school and college graduation are accepted expectations; when job skills and employment opportunities abound; when all people have quality, affordable health care; and where JESUS CHRIST IS LORD!"

A VISION STATEMENT IS WHAT WE HOPE WILL RESULT FROM THE ACCOMPLISHMENT OF THE MISSION.

Finally, each year we choose a theme and a verse, both of which reflect our larger mission. For example, 2012 is the Year of Justice and the year verse is Micah 6:8: "He has shown all you people what is good. And what does the LORD require of you? To act justly and to love mercy and to walk humbly with your God" (*TNIV*).

Ideally, each organizational entity within the larger ministry will have its own vision and mission statements in order to provide focus.

So, for example, LCC's development corporation, health center and legal center each have their own, individualized mission statements, all of which of course are consistent with LCC's overall mission.

EACH ORGANIZATIONAL ENTITY WITHIN THE LARGER MINISTRY SHOULD HAVE ITS OWN VISION AND MISSION STATEMENTS IN ORDER TO PROVIDE FOCUS.

All of these elements communicate to those in the church, including those who are being developed as leaders, that we are not simply wandering in the wilderness without a clear direction and with no goals in mind. It enables people to push in the same direction toward goals that have been carefully considered and clearly communicated.

## The Priority of Love

Mission and vision statements reflect what is distinctive about a church and its context. So, for example, a mission that includes economic empowerment would likely be more relevant in an inner-city (as opposed to a wealthy suburban) context. But regardless of context, *all* churches are called to love their neighborhoods. Every church ought to be seen as a lover of its community.

Thus, whenever people come to us asking for advice, our first response is to advise them to develop a greater love for those around them. We don't spoon-feed anyone; rather, we try to point them in the right direction. We encourage them to grapple with the implications of Scripture verses such as Isaiah 61:1: "The LORD has anointed me to preach good news to the poor. He has sent me to bind up the brokenhearted, to proclaim freedom for the captives and release from darkness for the prisoners." We might also recommend Wayne's book *Who Is My Neighbor?* for individual or group devotions.

It's best that this process not be shortchanged. We recommend that churches wanting to embark on a new path begin by spending at least

six months focusing on how to demonstrate love for those around them—on how they can embrace the reality that our love for Christ is revealed in our service to "the least of these" (Matt. 25:40). For churches that want to grow in this area, loving neighbors ought to become the focus for preaching, Sunday School, and virtually all other aspects of the church's life.

## Taking Stock

After a church or ministry comes to grips with the priority of love and develops a strong and growing desire to love their community, the next step is to bring the people of the community—not just church people, but the entire community—together to take stock of the community's strengths and weaknesses. Listening sensitively to the deepest cries of the people is a biblical concept. That's what the prophets did. It's what Jesus did.

LISTENING SENSITIVELY TO THE DEEPEST CRIES OF THE PEOPLE IS A BIBLICAL CONCEPT. IT'S WHAT JESUS DID.

Call the people together for a community meeting. Spread the word; put up posters. If you are located in an urban setting, a good rule of thumb is to cover a five-block radius around your church. Remember that you are most concerned about engaging the grassroots, as opposed to the "big shots." Don't worry about getting more people there than you can handle. Chances are that won't happen. (If it does, it will be a nice problem to have.) Most likely you will end up with somewhere between 25 and 50 people. By and large, they will be people who are highly invested in their community and committed to taking positive action.

It's fine to open and close in prayer, but remember that this is not an evangelistic session. It's a community meeting. The initial goal is to

listen. There are no right or wrong answers. Organizers of the effort are facilitators, not bosses or final decision makers.

Sit in a circle so it's clear that no one person or group is in charge. Start by listing your community's assets. Write them on a chalkboard or on newsprint. What are the good things about your neighborhood? What are its strengths? What do the people like about it? What are they proud of? Spend a little bit of time celebrating what is positive, perhaps by publicly acknowledging the people and organizations responsible for the good things mentioned.

Continue by making a list of those things that need to improve in your community. What do people not like? What are the most significant problems or challenges? What are people afraid of? What do they most want to see change?

## Begin with Small Steps

After taking stock, it's time to take action. Don't be overwhelmed by the length or the content of the list of things you want to change. Never think that your church or ministry is too small to accomplish anything significant. Truth be told, the smaller you are, the more flexible and agile you can be, making it easier to achieve goals.

Don't try to do everything at once. Those who try to accomplish everything sometimes end up accomplishing nothing. At Lawndale, we are still chipping away at the list we made all the way back in 1978. The important thing is not to finish the list; what matters is that the community is working together to address issues that affect neighborhood residents' quality of life.

One of the things people noted at one of our early community meetings was that there was a dangerous intersection in the neighborhood. People were getting hit (or coming close to getting hit) by cars. We gathered signatures and petitioned the city for a stop sign. The effort succeeded, proving to everyone that if we took action, things could change. So pick an item from your list and work on it. Small things will lead to bigger things.

When communities organize in this fashion, one of the results is that new leaders will step to the fore. They are usually not the leaders who are paid to find answers. They are people who lead from the heart,

not based on their self-interest. These leaders aren't appointed or elected; instead they emerge as people work together and things begin to happen spontaneously, not according to some carefully orchestrated plan. Eventually, decisions will have to be made—perhaps by consensus or vote. Regardless of what is decided, it is important to make sure all participants feel that their voices and perspectives have been heard, even when (*especially* when) they don't get their way. This can be done as part of the process of explaining all the considerations that went into a particular decision.

REGARDLESS OF WHAT IS DECIDED, MAKE SURE ALL PARTICIPANTS FEEL THEIR VOICES AND PERSPECTIVES HAVE BEEN HEARD, EVEN WHEN THEY DON'T GET THEIR WAY.

After a community meeting, the church or ministry might want to meet on their own to talk about what they have heard and to determine how to support whatever initiatives have been decided upon.

## Handling Criticism

There is no such thing as a leader who has never been criticized. As we noted earlier, almost everyone is a leader of someone. Do you know of a parent who has never been criticized by his or her children?

All leaders have their detractors. Criticism comes with the territory of leadership. So the question is not whether we will be criticized, but rather how we will deal with it.

Good leaders—those who are secure in their abilities, their motives and their call to lead—actually invite criticism. Keep in mind that although "criticism" has negative connotations, it can be a positive thing. If we are going to improve, we need others to point out to us what we are doing wrong.

Good leaders are themselves critics. Earlier, we pointed out some examples of Jesus being very candid with His disciples when they came up short. Good leaders strive to create an environment in which

people will tell the truth, including the truth about one another's shortcomings, but do so in a spirit of deep love and full support. When most of what you say to a person is positive and affirming, that person will not mind hearing a word or two about how to improve. In fact, he or she will likely thank you for it.

Even in an environment where criticism is accepted as normal, it's best to follow the maxim "Affirm publicly; critique privately." In other words, leaders who feel they have to critique someone for some reason should go to them privately. In turn, leaders have every right to expect this same treatment from those who are critiquing them.

Let's acknowledge, however, that not everybody plays by these rules. Leaders regularly face criticism—sometimes in public settings—that is not based on accurate facts and that is not offered in a kind, supportive way. The childhood saying, "Sticks and stones will break my bones, but words will never hurt me" is completely untrue. Words *can* hurt. In particular, they can hurt those who are sensitive, caring people—as servant leaders generally are.

WORDS CAN HURT THOSE WHO ARE SENSITIVE, CARING PEOPLE—AS SERVANT LEADERS GENERALLY ARE.

The first thing for a leader to do when someone is critical is take it in. Receive it. Don't be defensive. Thank the person for pointing out an area of concern. You can do this without saying that you agree with the criticism. But don't dismiss what's being said out of hand. Sometimes criticism, regardless of how it is offered, can be painful because it is true, or at least carries an element of truth. So consider it. Go back into your cave and reflect on it. Talk with other people, including your spouse and others who are closest to you and who will not hesitate to tell it like it is. We all have blind spots, so we need people we trust to help us distinguish between accurate and inaccurate criticism. Look for the possible truth in what critics are saying, and, if necessary, change what ought to be changed.

All this said, however, most leaders will have a few folks around them who are overly critical—people who seem to think that their mission in life is to find fault with everyone in the world except themselves. Being the target of such persons can be very draining. It can consume much-needed time and energy. God loves these people, too, but leaders are well advised to take steps to shield themselves from criticism that is unfair, unreasonable, unkind, or some combination of the three. One way to do this is by ignoring criticism that is anonymous. If you get a letter, check to see who wrote it. If it's anonymous and the first sentence is negative, throw it away. If someone wants to help you through their criticism, they have the responsibility to present their concerns to you openly.

LEADERS ARE WELL ADVISED TO TAKE STEPS TO SHIELD THEMSELVES FROM CRITICISM THAT IS UNFAIR, UNREASONABLE AND UNKIND,

In this technological age, some people have learned to use various messaging systems to create one-way conversations with the target of their criticism. For instance, people have figured out that if they call my (Wayne's) office after hours, they can get through to my voicemail instead of being greeted by a person. This gives them an opportunity to deliver their diatribe, without giving me a chance to respond.

In one instance, I met with a person who had been sending me frequent, negative emails and voicemails. I told this person that I was willing to meet face to face to discuss the issues. But I added that I was no longer going to listen to any critical voicemails or read any critical emails. I told this person, "As soon as I realize it's negative, I'm hitting the delete button, so it will be a total waste of your time. But I am willing to talk with you in person."

It can be particularly frustrating to have to deal with criticism whose source is unclear. For example, people may tell you what someone else has said or what other people are saying. As a variation on this theme, people will sometimes try to involve you in their criticism

of others or want you to take their side in a dispute with someone else. Don't do it. Say to that person, "If you have something against somebody, go straight to that person and try to resolve the issue."

Then there are those who don't criticize directly, but do so indirectly by complaining, perhaps because they disagree with some decision the church has made. Church leadership regularly has to make decisions about issues on which people in the congregation have opposing opinions: the times of the church services, the structure of church services, remodeling the sanctuary, and more. Some people, when they don't get their way, resort to complaining instead of accepting the decision and moving on.

For the sake of the larger mission, the church has no room for chronic complainers. In fact, it's better for people to leave than to complain constantly. I (Wayne) have told people on occasion, "If you can grow more and serve better in another church, feel free to go there. There are no bars on our doors. Don't complain; just leave. We don't need complainers."

Once again, the best defense against unfair criticism (and chronic complaining) is to be proactive by creating an environment in which criticism is welcome—within the bounds of clearly communicated attitudes and policies, and with loving one another as the ultimate goal. Keep in mind that people who are overly critical are often dealing with pain in their lives that has not been addressed or resolved. So even as you take steps to protect yourself and the integrity of the ministry, look for opportunities to meet people at their points of need.

## Church Discipline

Unfortunately, leaders sometimes have to deal with challenges they would rather not address—but which they must address if the ministry is to have integrity. People fail. While we worship a God who forgives—and believe that we are called to forgive as well—we also recognize that restoration requires genuine repentance and that indiscretion requires discipline.

It stands to reason that those who grew up without the benefit of loving parents and stable families will find it harder to follow the rules of society and of the Church. It's not easy for some people to simply

do the right thing. Ministry requires patience and the willingness to forgive as people struggle with this. That does not mean, however, that anything goes. Leaders face the challenge of dealing constructively with behavior that does not meet the ministry's ethical standards, and this sometimes necessitates discipline.

LEADERS FACE THE CHALLENGE OF DEALING CONSTRUCTIVELY WITH BEHAVIOR THAT DOES NOT MEET THE MINISTRY'S ETHICAL STANDARDS, AND THIS SOMETIMES NECESSITATES DISCIPLINE.

For church discipline to function well, the church first of all must be completely clear regarding what is expected of board members, staff and members. One of the ways we communicate expectations at Lawndale is by requiring that everyone who is part of the church staff sign an "Agreement of Responsibility." The statement specifies that each person working for the church "should demonstrate that he/she is a new creature in Christ, demonstrating a sincere desire for the Word of God and a desire to grow and mature in his/her daily walk with Christ." The page-long agreement also addresses specific behaviors and attitudes:

> In light of Biblical principles, the following practices are not acceptable: drunkenness; the use of illicit drugs; stealing; use of profane language; all forms of dishonesty including lying; cheating; [and] sexual sins such as participation in premarital sex, adulterous relationships and homosexual relationships. . . . Every staff member . . . is encouraged to maintain a healthy, positive attitude towards his or her job. Behaviors which are inconsistent with this attitude include: greed, jealousy, pride, lust, bitterness, needless anger, an unforgiving spirit, harmful discrimination and prejudices.

The agreement also states that staff members are to support the church and its other ministries. They, along with board members, are expected to be generous givers.

It's happened a lot over the years that people don't live up to these expectations. In these cases, we have taken action to guard the moral integrity of the ministry.

The goal is always repentance and full restoration of the individual. The first challenge is to determine whether a person's repentance is genuine. Sensitive leaders who know their people are usually able to tell. There are several indicators. If the violation is something that occurred only once or twice (as opposed to regularly over an extended period of time), it suggests genuine repentance. Does the person accept responsibility for the failure, or does he or she blame others for what happened? Has the offender taken (or is he or she willing to take) action to heal any relationships with those who were in some way hurt by the impropriety? Finally, is the person willing to be disciplined—to pay the penalty for what she or he has done?

There is no formula for what the discipline should be, or for how restoration should be handled. Each situation is unique. Restoration generally should not be public—although in some cases, if the offense is widely known and rumors are spreading, it is in the best interests of everyone to make it public.

THERE IS NO FORMULA FOR WHAT THE DISCIPLINE SHOULD BE, OR FOR HOW RESTORATION SHOULD BE HANDLED. EACH SITUATION IS UNIQUE.

The rule of thumb at Lawndale for someone who has failed to live up to his or her leadership responsibilities is a year out of leadership. Sometimes a person has to be fired from his or her job. But again, each situation is different.

There are a few principles, however, that don't change. First is the mandate to continue to love the person, no matter what he or she has done. Next, take your time. It's better to make a good decision than to act too hastily. Seek guidance, especially from those who are a little older and have had more experience in dealing with these situations. As stated throughout this book, good leaders seek advice. You can do

this without revealing the details of a particular situation. But never make a decision in isolation—and never make a big decision if you're the only one who thinks it's the right thing to do. The bigger the decision, the more you must be sure it's right, and decisions related to church discipline are huge ones.

CHAPTER SIXTEEN

# PARTING WORDS OF HOPE

Wise people recognize that the goal of parenting is for mothers and fathers to work themselves out of a job—to bring their children to a place where they no longer need their parents, though they continue to love them. The same is true for those who are developing leaders. I (John) have spent most of my life developing leaders and Christian community development ministries—and then walking away from them. (Sometimes people thought I walked away too soon, but I knew that the new leaders were ready to spread their wings.)

THE GOAL FOR DEVELOPING LEADERS IS TO WORK OURSELVES OUT OF A JOB—TO BRING THEM TO A PLACE WHERE THEY NO LONGER NEED US.

I did this first in Mendenhall, Mississippi, during the 1960s and early '70s (The Mendenhall Ministries). I did the same thing in Jackson (Voice of Calvary Ministries) in the '70s and early '80s, and then in Pasadena, California (Harambee Christian Family Center), from 1982 until my return to Jackson in 1996. Though the specific outreach efforts differ, in each place Christian ministry continues.

I'm in my eighties now, and I know that my time on this earth is limited, and that God will be calling me home in the not-too-distant future. So I'm doing one last time what I've been doing all along, namely turning over the leadership of the Spencer Perkins Center (named to honor my late son), located in Jackson, to others. Through faith, I have confidence the things God has allowed me to start will not just continue, but will also grow as leaders I've developed become developers of leaders themselves.

This approach lies at the heart of CCDA's approach to community development. With each passing year, new leaders and ministries are emerging that are changing their communities in the name of Jesus Christ—and CCDA's influence is by no means limited to the United States. For example, an Ethiopian woman named Jember Teferra, who has been coming to CCDA events for 20 years, has launched two sig-

nificant community development ministries in poverty-stricken neighborhoods of Addis Ababa.

Developing leaders requires persistence. It's been said that the first rule of advertising is "Repeat, repeat, repeat." This rule tops all others because marketers have learned through extensive experience that, like it or not, it takes repetition and reinforcement to get a message through successfully. The same is true in leadership development. You may need to share the principles and insights you have learned many times before those you are developing fully grasp them and begin to apply them in their own leadership efforts. In that spirit, we are taking the opportunity to review a few key themes here before offering some final words of encouragement and hope.

## It Starts (and Ends) with Love

Christian leadership is ultimately all about love. It's about loving God and God's kingdom. It's about loving our neighbors as ourselves. It's about loving our enemies, as hard as that can be. It's about loving those we are leading, including those with a few (or more than a few) "rough edges." It's about loving those whom we are developing as leaders, which sometimes requires a ton of patience.

In short, the goal of the Christian leader—indeed the goal of all Christians—ought to be to love every human being we meet. "A new command I give you," Jesus told His disciples. "Love one another. As I have loved you, so you must love one another" (John 13:34).

THE GOAL OF THE CHRISTIAN LEADER OUGHT TO BE TO LOVE EVERY HUMAN BEING WE MEET.

With this in mind, it helps to view our lives through the lens of gratitude for the love we have received from God. Many know 1 John 4:19—"we love because he first loved us"—as the "gratitude verse." Our goal becomes to live every moment of our lives joyfully and with thanks for

the love we have received—a love whose depths we are not capable of fully comprehending. As we do that, our love for those around us increases to reflect, more and more, the love we have experienced.

Love, of course, has an emotional dimension to it. That is, love is something we feel. We feel different kinds of love in various situations—and that emotion can be very powerful. But love for our neighbors and our world will never be enough if it remains confined to the realm of emotion. Genuine love compels us to take action to bring hope and healing to our world. It requires that we exercise our leadership gifts and help others to develop and exercise their gifts as well.

## The Priority of Humility

The approach to leadership that we have presented in these pages is built around humility—counting others as higher than ourselves. Servant leadership places the needs of other people above our own desire for credit and recognition. A humble approach to leadership enables us to build a culture based on teamwork and common goals, as opposed to top-down organizational charts. The best leaders are people who don't need to be—and don't want to be—in charge of everything. Instead, they aspire to spread authority and responsibility around. Along with this, they encourage others to express themselves freely—to say what's on their minds and allow their voices to be heard without fear of adverse consequences.

Servant leaders who are motivated by humility increase their capacity to influence not through power plays motivated by organizational politics, but by working alongside others in the trenches. The best leaders are not just leaders but doers as well.

## Leadership Development

A commitment to servant leadership flows naturally to an emphasis on developing other leaders. After all, the job of building the Kingdom is too big and too important to be assigned to just a handful of people. Everyone is to be involved at some level. Servant leaders are team players, completely willing to give away power for the ultimate, long-range good of the mission.

Developing others as leaders begins with helping them to recognize that they already are leaders—or at least potential leaders—who have the opportunity to, as the saying goes, "bloom where they have been planted." Thus, those who come forward and say they want to expand their leadership territory—their realms of influence—can be encouraged to lead right where they are. In keeping with the message of Jesus' Parable of the Talents, people ought to demonstrate that they can succeed in managing a few things before they are put in charge of many (see Matt. 25:14-30).

SERVANT LEADERS ARE TEAM PLAYERS, COMPLETELY WILLING TO GIVE AWAY POWER FOR THE ULTIMATE, LONG-RANGE GOOD OF THE MISSION.

It's fair and reasonable to expect developing leaders to pay their dues. A woman who is leading a Girl Scout troop today should not expect to become a U.S. Senator next week—although perhaps she will become one in time. The apostle Paul made it clear that people should not be placed in positions of leadership in the Early Church too quickly. They needed some seasoning. They had to prove themselves, not only in terms of moral integrity, but also with regard to the ability to manage. In 1 Timothy 3:4-5, Paul writes that an overseer "must manage his own family well and see that his children obey him with proper respect. (If anyone does not know how to manage his own family, how can he take care of God's church?)"

Those who aspire to be leaders ultimately have responsibility for their own development. The same applies to all current leaders. We ought to be reading books; going to seminars and workshops; and listening to and learning from those, including mentors, who can contribute to our development. Remember that developing as a leader is a lifelong endeavor.

It's important for those of us who are developing other leaders to recognize that we are role models. Sometimes we are aware that we're being watched and imitated. Many times we are not. Developers of

leaders also long to be mentors. We survey the landscape around us and identify a few people in whom we want to invest our lives in a special way. We seek to teach and nurture these people at every turn. We are aware of their needs and life goals; we regard them as family.

Developers of leaders never give up on people, even in the midst of failure and disappointment. We recognize that not all future leaders begin at the same starting point. Some need a little more time, perhaps because they did not receive a solid educational foundation or had no access to positive role models, even in their families. Thus, developing leaders sometimes requires heavy doses of compassion, empathy and patience.

## An Encouraging Word

The Christian Community Development Association uses the following poem, whose origins are not known for certain, as a philosophical guide to its mission. (The two italicized lines are additions, courtesy of John.)

Go to the people
Live among them
Learn from them
*Listen to them*
*Labor with them*
Love them
Start with what they know
Build on what they have
But of the best leaders
When their task is done
The people will remark,
"We have done it ourselves."

This brief poem captures the essence of servant leadership and leadership development. Success is not simply about coming up with a strategic master plan, applying basic leadership principles to carry it out, basking in the glow of success, and then moving on to a more prestigious position at a bigger organization to address greater chal-

lenges for a larger salary and a more luxurious company car. That's the way things work in the corporate world, but not in the Kingdom.

THE MISSION OF SERVANT LEADERS IS NOT SIMPLY TO ACCOMPLISH SPECIFIC GOALS BUT TO SHARE LIFE, LEADERSHIP, POWER AND RESPONSIBILITY WITH OTHERS.

To be sure, as we've acknowledged, many leadership principles from the business world do apply in the context of Christian ministry. But the difference—and it's a big one—is that the mission of servant leaders is not simply to accomplish specific goals. It's to share life and leadership and power and responsibility with others until they are able to say, with the pride that results from significant accomplishment, "Nobody did this for us. We did not sit idly by and let others solve our problems and address our challenges. We made the sacrifices. We paid the price. We didn't give up when things got tough. We have done it ourselves. And the future of our ministry and our community is better for it." This is the approach the leadership revolution requires.

The road ahead will not always be smooth. In fact, most of the time it will be rugged. We will go through long stretches without seeing much, if any, fruit. Those who minister in the context of the so-called permanent underclass will likely find ministry to be especially challenging much of the time. Young people we've known and loved will be randomly gunned down in the street. People we were convinced had overcome their addiction to drugs or alcohol will relapse into old patterns of behavior. Children will grow up having known their fathers only from the other side of a prison window. People we've developed as leaders, in whom we've invested considerable amounts of time and energy and placed a large measure of hope, will leave the community, never to return except for an occasional visit. That's okay. There should be no strings attached to those we are mentoring and developing. They will follow God's call wherever it takes them. Still, it's disappointing. We accept it and take the next step forward, but it's hard—very hard.

As leaders, we will fail—many times. We will let people down, including the people we care about most in this world. Sometimes we will attempt to solve a problem or address a challenge and come up short. We might even make things worse. But good leaders turn failures into learning opportunities. A difficult problem serves only to increase the determination to solve it. As Martin Luther King Jr. wrote in reference to the failed efforts at desegregation in Albany, Georgia, in the early 1960s, "There were weaknesses in Albany. . . . Each of us expected that setbacks would be a part of the ongoing effort. . . . Human beings . . . must make mistakes and learn from them, make more mistakes and learn anew. They must taste defeat as well as success, and discover how to live with each. Time and action are the teachers."[1]

BUT GOOD LEADERS TURN FAILURES INTO LEARNING OPPORTUNITIES. A DIFFICULT PROBLEM SERVES ONLY TO INCREASE THE DETERMINATION TO SOLVE IT.

Despite the challenges, failures and disappointments that are sure to accompany a leadership revolution, we won't give up. We will press on in obedience and in response to God's call on our lives. Those of us who are committed to transforming our communities are in it for the long haul. More often than not, instead of moving on to "bigger and better" things because of success, we will remain despite the absence of success—or at least, the absence of readily visible success. We would do well to remind ourselves and our co-laborers that it might be our mission to plant seeds for others to water and for still others, in time, to harvest.

For those who have been called by God, there is no alternative but to press on. We can do nothing else—and that's a good thing. For beyond the challenges, there awaits great joy in seeing people—many of whom will remind us of ourselves—who are willing to follow where God leads despite the dangers, toils and snares they will likely encounter along the way. These courageous men and women, who are

willing to risk everything for the sake of following Christ, are the future of the leadership revolution.

In a culture in which many well-to-do children are disappointed at Christmastime because they didn't get everything they wanted, there is joy in seeing children smile as a result of receiving gifts, however small, that they never expected. There is joy in seeing young people who had the entire deck of life stacked against them be embraced by a caring community and grow up to become mature, faithful, daring, ambitious disciples of Christ. We've been watching this happen for nearly 40 years now—children becoming teenagers; then young adults; then loving husbands and wives, fathers and mothers; and leaders in their church, workplaces and community. What a joy it is to see someone we knew when he or she was in diapers going off to college!

Many churches in America are struggling to survive. Some are having to join with other churches or close their doors altogether. According to a March 2012 Gallup poll on religious behavior in the United States, "32% of Americans are nonreligious, based on their statement that religion is not an important part of their daily life and that they seldom or never attend religious services."[2]

That's almost a third of Americans who now report that they seldom or never go to a religious house of worship—and there are those who contend that this percentage would be much higher if it were based on actual behavior as opposed to self-reporting.

It's not just about numbers. The Church's influence (or lack thereof) on our culture's morality, including morality as it relates to how our society cares for its weakest, most vulnerable people, is a cause for concern.

It's important for us to recognize that if we are to make a difference, following Christ must go beyond simply maintaining an organization. Perhaps people (especially idealistic and energetic youth) are leaving or staying away from the Church not because it's too hard, but because it's too easy. Perhaps it's not because they have too much to do, but because they don't have enough—not enough meaning, not enough relevance, not enough pain, not enough challenge, not enough struggle—and way too much comfort.

We will grow through embracing more challenge, more struggle, more meaning, more sacrificial love—and even more pain. We will

experience more joy. *We need a revolution.* Won't you join us? Let's develop the people who are among us today so that they can become the leaders of tomorrow.

**Notes**

1. Martin Luther King Jr., *Why We Can't Wait* (Boston: Beacon Press, 2010), p. 41.
2. Frank Newport, "Mississippi Is Most Religious State," March 27, 2012. http://www.gallup.com/poll/153479 mississippi-religious-state.aspx (accessed July 2012).

## Also Available from Regal Books

# FOLLOW ME TO FREEDOM

by Shane Claiborne and John M. Perkins

ISBN-10: 0-8307-5120-3
ISBN-13: 978-0-8307-5120-4

Shane Claiborne and John Perkins know the hopes and longings of this age. One is young; the other is decades older. One is a self-proclaimed reformed redneck who now lives in the inner city and has become a voice for compassionate change; the other is an evangelical African-American voice for civil rights who once was almost beaten to death by police in Mississippi and went on to counsel three presidents and launch a reconciliation movement. You would be hard pressed to find a more unlikely duo, yet Claiborne and Perkins now lead the way toward freedom for all. In a world hungry for radical hope, their stories, lessons learned and wisdom will guide us as we walk down the rugged road to another world. Followers of Christ will not only be inspired, but also catalyzed into being the hands, feet and heart of real change—and the world will never be the same.

Come along as we live out this conversation . . . there are many obstacles—so much suffering, poverty and violence. But our God is familiar with suffering. Our God can swallow up armies and pour out bread from the heavens. Wall Street may fail us, but the God who takes care of the lilies and the sparrows will never let us down. Our Savior has stared evil in the face and overcome it with love. And now we are invited to join the triumph of the cross . . . and to lead others on the narrow, rugged road to freedom."

**Turn the page to read the introduction to *Follow Me to Freedom*!**

# AN INTRODUCTION

**SHANE:** I was introduced to John Perkins when I read his book *Let Justice Roll Down*. He opened my eyes and set my heart on fire as he told how he had responded to extreme racism and hatred with forgiveness and love.

John showed no fear as a civil rights leader in the Deep South in the late 1960s, when everything, including his life, was on the line. He modeled being an ordinary radical before I even knew the term. Not even halfway through the book, I knew John Perkins was a leader I wanted to follow.

Not so long after that, John and I met. He came down to visit our little experiment in community on the north side of Philadelphia. I remember wanting to give John an impressive tour of our nonprofit organization, but all he wanted to do was sit on the steps in front of our building and eat ice cream with the kids. He had been on plenty of snazzy tours of ministries that were going to "transform the world" and just wanted to meet our friends here in the neighborhood.

I remember later that day whining to John about how we had been working so hard and hadn't seen much of anything get better. There were still gunshots all the time—there was still heroine, there was still prostitution, there was still poverty, there was still pain. I remember complaining, "It's been over three years and there aren't many signs of change." John looked me dead in the eye and, with the gentleness of a father, plainly and so sincerely explained the way things work: "Oh, Shane, you'll start to see some things change. You'll start to see signs of transformation—in about 10 years. Or maybe 12." And he didn't flinch. That was his promise: We'd see change *in 10 or 12 years*. I gulped. That was nearly half my life up to that moment, yet somehow I knew he spoke the truth, and it gave me hope.

John's was (and is) the voice of someone who has committed his life to a movement that requires deep faith and revolutionary patience, who has set his hand to the plow and hasn't looked back. That's someone I want to rub off on me . . . so I followed.

John soon invited me to join up with the Christian Community Development Association (CCDA),[1] one of the few organizations that

crosses the generational divide with a relentless conviction that the old and young must dream together. It's an incredible family that has been practicing resurrection and paving the way to freedom in some of the toughest corners of our world.

*John*: A few years back, I started hearing rumors about Shane. You might have heard some too. Word was going around that a group of mostly young white middle-class Christians, led by a guy who dressed like a monk, had stirred up things on the north side of Philadelphia. All the fuss started when the Roman Catholic Archdiocese threatened to evict some homeless families from a boarded-up church building where they had taken refuge. Shane and his college buddies were rightly outraged, became squatters with the families and risked arrest. Once better housing was found for the families, instead of retreating back to the suburbs, Shane and his friends stayed on. They could have swept into the struggling neighborhood, offered a cure to the immediate crisis, left some boxes of food and departed with smiles on their faces. They could have returned to their college campuses, written papers on their inner-city triumph and been heroes. Instead, Shane and some of his friends did the unthinkable by joining in with the people: they felt the pain, saw the need for more and made North Philly their home too.[2] I admit it: I liked what I had heard, and I was curious.

So, I arranged a trip to Philadelphia to see things firsthand. By then, Shane and his friends had created The Simple Way—an intentional community that is part of what is now being called the new monastic movement.[3] They pooled their resources and committed themselves to doing life together. In a small way they remind me of myself when, decades earlier, I moved my family from the suburbs of Southern California back to my native Mississippi, at the height of the civil rights movement.

Sure enough, Shane and I sat on the stoop in front of his building on Potter Street, eating ice cream with the kids. You can learn a lot about a person when you watch him in his environment, and you can learn even more when you observe him interact with the children. You know what I saw? In Shane, I sensed the most humble, sensible, kind radical you will ever meet. His unusual dress and quiet manner disarm you. But you immediately know there is more going on inside.

He actually listens—tenderly listens, not just to your words, but also to your heart. He asks probing questions and wants real answers too.

There on the stoop, my ice cream melting, I could see concern and love pour out from Shane for the folks in his neighborhood—a deep love—and I could see his neighbors respond with respect for him. He reminded me a little of my oldest son, Spencer, who like Shane had so much hope that things could be better for the poor. Spencer led a little community in Jackson, Mississippi, but a few years ago he suffered cardiac arrest. I really think he died of a broken heart—shattered because he saw the need and had the passion but was unable to do more. Spencer would have found Shane's revolution irresistible. It would have given him hope, and he would have joined in.

Right away, I could see that Shane was not a crazy cult leader but a prophetic voice—and I knew he was someone we needed to join in with us. At CCDA, we had talked a lot about how to keep the vision of reconciliation and community development moving forward, how to pass it along to the younger generation. We invited Shane to be on the CCDA board of directors, and we have become stronger, richer, deeper people because of his involvement. Now the demands of his travel schedule make it hard for him to attend board meetings, but we still need his presence and his voice, so he is on our board of advisors.

Not only has CCDA grown from Shane's example, but people respond to him at the Urbana missions conference, Westmont College, the National Pastor's Conference, and pretty much wherever he goes. They get excited about his story and embrace his challenges; after all, Shane is cool. He is real. But he really connects with people when they see that he doesn't just do things *for* the poor; rather, he has a charisma *with* the poor.

Shane and his friends went to North Philly, not saying, "Here we are to lift you up," but saying, "Here we are to become one with you." Historically, a big divide has separated blacks and whites—and there hasn't been a deep enough commitment to fill the gap. Whites typically come alongside blacks for a little while and then leave. Shane and The Simple Way are there to stay. They also do life a little different. No one can ever accuse them of being a typical nonprofit, dependent upon a denomination, foundation or church for funding. Because of their simple lifestyle and because they have not presented themselves

as a source of material goods in North Philly, they do not have the same interdependencies as some others. They are free to be more radical and lean on Jesus.

I know Shane will not want me saying all of this about him.

SHANE: Amen to that.

John: But this is my part of this book, so I get to do some talking. One time, Shane surprised and challenged folks at Willow Creek Community Church. Without any advance warning—so that people would have their best footwear on—he invited everyone to the altar to take off their shoes. And as you can imagine, at Willow Creek that meant a pretty big pile. The next week they gave the shoes out to people who needed them. Another time, at a CCDA board meeting in Atlanta, we discovered he wasn't staying at the nice hotel with the rest of us—by choice. At night, he quietly slipped away and camped out under a bridge with some homeless folks. That was a real wake-up call. He doesn't do these things to impress anyone, but he makes an impression. I am struck most by Shane's humility.

Today, we need humble and creative leaders—people who lead out of who they are. This new generation has not been infected so much by the historical racism and prejudices that have contaminated my own generation and the boomers—both blacks and whites. Shane is one of a new breed. He is an emerging leader that I am comfortable following. I don't know what the future will look like, but I know I want to tag along.

SHANE: You probably have already noticed that John and I are a little different from each other . . . *I have more hair.* Honestly, I am a recovering redneck from Eastern Tennessee; he is an elder statesman of the evangelical church from Mississippi. He was born before World War II was fought. I was born the year Saigon fell and the Vietnam War ended. He wears a suit and tie. I only wear a tie to hold my hair back . . . and since John busted me on my clothes a few pages back, let me say, my clothes are a little different because I make them with my momma each winter. I'm still working up to sewing the suit—you can call me an apprentice seamstress . . . or "tailor" I reckon (I think my

mom wanted a girl, but a boy who sews will have to suffice). John is married and has seven living adult children. I am still single (at least at the writing of this book!). He has counseled three presidents and has already been invited to the White House by Barack Obama. I had a different little campaign this last election: "Jesus for President" (more on that later). And so it goes. You'd be hard-fetched to find a more unlikely duo. While our pasts are about as different as you can get, the future that we invite you to imagine with us is almost identical.

*John*: The temptations faced, the stories told and the physical abilities at 30 years old are a little different from those we meet at 70-plus years, but that's part of the fun of this conversation.

**SHANE:** We have each made our share of mistakes and, hopefully, learned from them; but at the end of the day, even if by default, we have chosen to be leaders—or leadership has chosen us. It seems that the stuff we put our hands to bears fruit, and that people are following . . . or at least buying our books. Heck, someone even created a "fake Shane Claiborne" on Twitter that some people follow . . . and the funny thing is some people think that's actually me! And John probably has a Facebook fan club.

*John*: Funny, I really do have a Facebook page! My daughter Elizabeth put it up and keeps it going. But seriously, Shane is right. We are different. And I think that's part of what reconciliation is all about. If we cannot be reconciled with people that look different than we look, then what is reconciliation? And there will be no true freedom for any of us unless we are first reconciled to each other and to God.

**SHANE:** Most books on leadership have best-practice models, seven secrets to success or "amazing new" paradigms (and a fair amount of fluff, too, though I won't mention any specific titles). We certainly can learn from Maxwell, Blanchard, Stanley and others about leadership, but John and I cannot write a book that way. We speak not as consultants, but as friends in the struggle. We speak out of our lives in the trenches, from the broken streets of Jackson and North Philly, from the abandoned places of the empire in which we find ourselves. Don't get

me wrong: John could give you a list of "10 Ways to Transform Your Leadership" (and he probably will, and they will be magical). I, however, am just not that linear. So this will be fun.

It's also true that we wanted to write this together but have pretty wild lives (heck, we barely have time to read, much less write a book together), so our friends had a great idea: Rather than recycle material or try to physically sit down and write together, let's just get John and me together for a few hours here and a few more hours there and have some honest, raw conversations on "followership" and on leadership . . . and then turn our thoughts into a book. So here it is.

Most books by two authors are written in one voice. Nope. We decided that combining our voices would not only be difficult but would also be just plain odd (like mixing smooth jazz and punk rock and trying to dance to it). So we have chosen a unique format, trying to preserve both voices, doing a little harmonizing without homogenizing, and hoping it makes you dance. We each will tell our part of the story in our own voice, sometimes commenting on what the other says, sometimes not. Sometimes John will give a long teaching (because it is so good!), and other times (like right now) I will be carrying on. Like I said, this will be fun.

We have even sprinkled in a few blank places and numbers . . .

1. ______________________________

2. ______________________________

3. ______________________________

. . . so that those of you who just have to have outlines can create your own as you go along.

We both recognize that there are no easy answers, and books can only go so far . . . but this book is more about taking you on a journey than trying to get you to a destination. We do not offer a new theory or prescription, nor do we attempt a comprehensive study. Rather, we submit our experiences, our lessons learned and our unresolved questions, in a day and time that needs leaders and followers of integrity and action.

We hope that what you read feels like a conversation you'd have in rocking chairs on the porch, sipping sweet tea (perhaps not a bad place to read it either). John and I once sat on that stoop in Philadelphia eating ice cream and just being part of the neighborhood. He listened to my dreams, my hopes and my questions. In Mississippi, I visited John's home where he and Vera Mae have a historic Southern farmhouse they have renovated. On warm, humid summer nights, John likes to sit in a rocking chair, watch the sun set and tell stories of the past and the future.

John: *Follow Me to Freedom* is not just for leaders. It is for anyone who has ever led or followed, and for everyone who wants to. So join us now. Bring along your youthful dreams . . .

SHANE: . . . and your age-old wisdom. Let's sit together on the stoop on Potter Street in Philly, and on the porch of the farmhouse in Mississippi. No anecdotes or formulas . . . just a beautiful conversation. Come on.

Notes

1. For more information about CCDA, visit www.ccda.org.
2. For more of the story, see Shane Claiborne, *The Irresistible Revolution: Living as an Ordinary Radical* (Grand Rapids, MI: Zondervan, 2006).
3. To learn more about intentional communities, see Jonathan Wilson-Hartgrove, *New Monasticism: What It Has to Say to Today's Church* (Grand Rapids, MI: Brazos Press, 2008).

# ALSO AVAILABLE FROM

# WAYNE GORDON

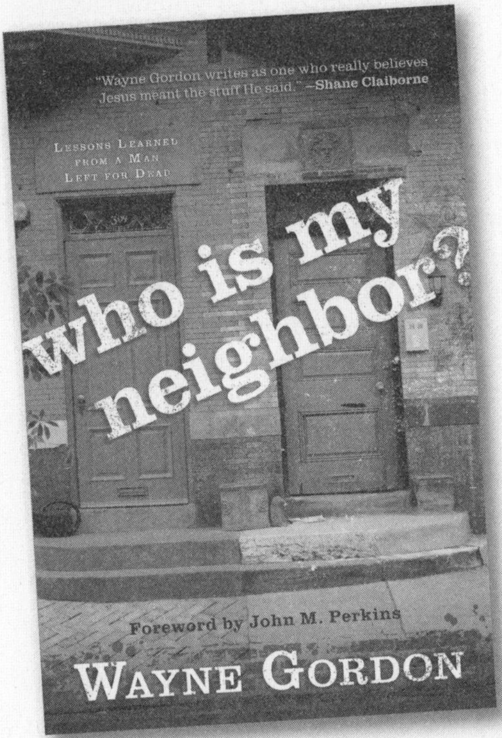


**Who Is My Neighbor?**
Wayne Gordon
ISBN 978.08307.57657
ISBN 08307.57651

When a lawyer asked Jesus, "Who is my neighbor?" (Luke 10:29), his question initiated an interesting conversation. Instead of offering the lawyer an exhaustive list of neighbors and non-neighbors, Jesus told a story . . . a tale we know as the Parable of the Good Samaritan. From that famous story, *Who Is My Neighbor?* draws more than 40 characteristics of the man who was beaten, robbed and left for dead on the road to Jericho—the character Jesus created to show His followers how to recognize our neighbors. Dr. Wayne Gordon brings the forsaken traveler vividly to life and shows you how to use Jesus' parable as a starting point for your relationships in your community and interactions with the world. As you catch Jesus' radical vision of what it means to be a Good Samaritan, you'll also find practical suggestions for meeting needs and changing the lives of those around you . . . that is, your neighbors!

## Available at Bookstores Everywhere!

Go to **www.regalbooks.com** to learn more about your favorite Regal books and authors. Visit us online today!

**Regal**
*God's Word for Your World*™
**www.regalbooks.com**

# AUTHOR CONTACT


## JOHN M. PERKINS

Visit the Perkins Leadership Retreat at the
John and Vera Mae Perkins Foundation
1831 Robinson St., Jackson, MS 39209

Email: info@jmpf.org
Phone: 601-354-1563
facebook.com/pages/John-M-Perkins-Foundation/40947699914
**www.jmpf.org**

## Wayne Gordon

Lawndale Community Church
3827 W. Ogden Ave.
Chicago, IL 60623

**www.lawndalechurch.org**

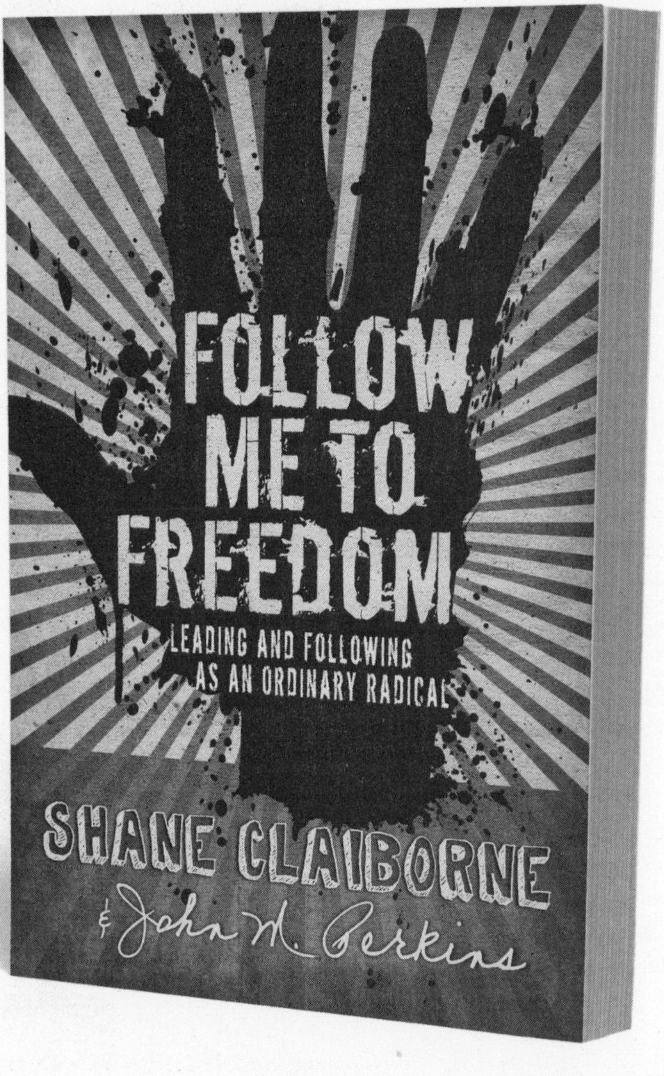


John M. Perkins & Wayne Gordon